Right to Education in India-
Inclusion, Impact and Way forward

Dr Vikas Mane

KALPAZ

ISBN: 978-93-5324-961-8

First Published, 2022

Published by

Kalpaz Publications
C-30, Satyawati Nagar,
Delhi – 110052
Ph.: 011-47034999, 9811692060
www.kalpazpublications.com
E-mail: kalpaz@hotmail.com

Printed at: Gyan Press, Delhi.

Contents

Preface

The right to education act 2009 is a revolutionary step towards universalisation of elementary education leading to a mainstreaming of all children towards a quality and holistic learning endeavour. This book written on the basis of a major research project sponsored by the Indian Council of Social Sciences Research, New Delhi provides an opportunity to delve into the various implementation issues of the Right of Children to Free and Compulsory Education Act, 2009, that include - admission process, no detention policy, 25 percent neighbourhood admission policy, continuous and comprehensive evaluation, social relationships in the class and school, role of the school management committees as people's representation in the functioning of the school, among others. Its implementation faces many issues regarding quality, quantity and inclusion especially regarding the SC and ST students. With a thorough probe of its implementation in two socio-economically contrasting districts and with international reference of similar educational right acts, a more comprehensive and socially inclusive act need be in place.

A special thanks to my institution, Indian Institute of Education, built and nurtured by the great educationists, Shri J. P. Naik and Dr Chitra Naik, for all it's support and cooperation. Special thanks are due to the Director of the Centre for Educational Studies. I am highly grateful to all.

I hope this book will be useful to students and teachers of education and the state policy makers and other agencies for effective implementation of an empirically enriched right to education act.

June 2022 **Dr Vikas Mane**

Pune

Abbreviations

AAAS –	Age Appropriate Admitted Students
Appls –	Applications
B. Ed –	Bachelor of Education
CCE –	Continuous and Comprehensive Evaluation
D. Ed –	Diploma in Education
DNT –	De-notified and Nomadic Tribe
HSC –	Higher Secondary School Certificate
ICT –	Information and Communication Technology
M. Phil –	Master of Philosophy
NA –	Not Applicable
NR –	No Response
NT –	Nomadic Tribe
OBC –	Other Backward Classes
RTE –	The Right of Children to Free and Compulsory Education Act, 2009
SC –	Scheduled Caste
SCERT –	State Council for Educational Research and Training
SLSM –	Special Learning Support Material
SMC –	School Management Committee.
SSC –	Secondary School Certificate
ST –	Scheduled Tribe
Ph. D –	Doctor of Philosophy
ZP –	Zilha Parishad

Chapter - I

Social Exclusion - Concept and Implications

(1) Introduction - The implementation of the Right of Children to Free and Compulsory Education Act, 2009 (RTE) is indeed a great compliance of Universal human rights and that of right to living under article 21 of the Indian Constitution that guarantees protection of life and personal liberty. The Right of Children to Free and Compulsory Education Act, 2009 (RTE) is the vehicle of the continuing objective of Universal elementary education in India. The Educational learning within its structural and systemic parts is certainly on tracks in India but it represents a learning which is formal and mainstream and possibly lacks in pedagogical and curricular diversity. The RTE has made mandatory infrastructural provisions for schools including buildings and grounds and mandatory affiliation to some affiliating school board along with the curriculum that is approved by a government body. These provisions obviously mean that alternate or experimental or mobile schools without infrastructural provisions or with distinctive pedagogy and content do not have space for survival under the RTE regime. Such schools are alternate efforts to plug the shortages of schools and educational diversity in India. They represent a different approach to life, to understanding and learning. They present diversity. And diversity is the essence of life. So, as good as the right to education is, it's obligatory and exclusivist nature is not the best and only solution for universal elementary education.

The compulsion of elementary education is generally, but subtly understood to be perpetuation of a culture. But we need to see the socio-economic and especially the economic outcomes of the prevailing culture. If the present culture is not good for progressive change there is need for change, and change can only come through variation. That is variety in the teaching - learning processes. Uniformity is an obstacle.

So, as important as infrastructure is, for a school, we need to keep space for spirited schools that are keen on running a different school, despite lack of complete infrastructure. The spirit, willingness and passion are important for holistic learning outcomes. Perpetuation only builds uniformity that lacks in verve and dynamism.

The noble idea of accommodating 25% of Economically Weaker Sections (EWS) students from the neighborhood is for the interface and dynamics of socio-cultural experiences between the elites and poor students besides imparting quality education to poor students. The understanding of each other's experiences and outlook for a better socio-economic understanding of the world and the sensitisation and holistic understanding for better student responses.

If this is the basic idea of this neighbourhood admission provision, an idea for dynamic interface, then it has to be formalised and substantiated. The strength of both the elite and the underprivileged students need to be exchanged dynamically. This dynamic interface needs to be incorporated into the school curriculum and activities. But in fact, the RTE Act talks much about the continuous and comprehensive evaluation rather than a continuous and comprehensive curriculum.

The character strengths and skill sets of the underprivileged students could be shared with other students and in turn receive the skill sets, confidence and smartness of the elite students.

This interface can be further taken into the pedagogy and curricula in the schools via Interdisciplinarity in the social sciences and pure sciences. This interdisciplinarity shall provide a holistic learning and changed sequence of understanding for children of concepts, processes and experiments, both from the social and science domains.

Community living in humanity has been in existence since time immemorial. The exigencies of survival, economic empowerment along social lines and a political framework for ordered living has been in existence for long. People live in communities and nation-states. But these Nation States were not ideal for equitable living. They eventually evolved into a stratified system of community living.

The nation states and communities with access to fertile land, natural resources and superior intellect led to a layered society, including more endowed and less so, sections of people.

Amartya Sen (2002) differentiated between active and passive exclusion. He defined Active exclusion as the deliberate exclusion of people from opportunity through government policy or other means. Passive exclusion as defined by him works through the social process in which there is no deliberate attempts to exclude, but never-the-less may result in exclusion from a set of circumstances.

These developments in social science literature enable us to understand the meaning and manifestations of the concept of social exclusion, and its applicability to caste -and ethnicity based exclusion in India. The dimensions involving the notion of exclusion are emphasized, namely the societal institutions of exclusion and their outcome in terms of depreciation. In order to understand the dimensions of exclusion it is necessary to understand the societal interrelations and institutions which lead to exclusion of certain groups and deprivation in multiple spheres –civil, cultural, political and economic. Thus, for a broader understanding of the concept of exclusion an insight into the societal processes and institutions of exclusion is as important as the outcome and terms of depreciation for certain groups.

Theoretical formulations by social scientists recognised that in its essential form caste as a system of social and economic governance or organisation of production and distribution is governed by certain customary rules and norms which are unique and distinct. The organisational scheme of the caste system is based on the division of people into social groups or castes in which the civil, cultural and economic rights of each individual caste are predetermined or described by Burke and made hereditary. Thus, allotment of civil, cultural and economic rights is therefore unequal and hierarchical. The most important feature of the caste system however, is that it provides for a regulatory mechanism to enforce the social and economic organisation through the instruments of social ostracism by way of social fines and penalties. The caste system is reinforced further with justification and support from philosophical elements in the Hindu religion.

The caste systems fundamental characteristic of fixed civil, cultural and economic rights for each caste with restrictions for change implies obligatory exclusion of one caste from the rights of another caste or from undertaking the occupations of other castes. Exclusion and discrimination in civil, cultural and particularly in economic spheres is therefore internal to the system and unnecessary outcome of its governing principles. In the market economy framework, occupational immobility would operate through restrictions in various markets such as land, labour, credit and services necessary for any economic activity. Labour, being an integral part of production process of any community activity would obviously become a part of market discrimination.

The practice of caste based exclusion, though diminishing, has been prevalent in India over centuries. It involves failure of access and entitlements not only to economic rights but also to civil, cultural and political rights. Involves what has been described as living mode exclusion. Caste untouchability and ethnicity based exclusion does reflect the inability of individuals and groups like untouchables adivasi and similar groups to interact freely and productively with others and to take part in the full economic social and political life of a community. Incomplete citizenship or denial of civil rights such as freedom of expression, rule of law, right to justice, political rights like right and means to participate in the exercise of political power and socio-economic rights comprising of economic security and equality of opportunities are key to impoverished lives.

1.1 Inclusiveness

Rene Lenoir is credited with the authorship of the term social exclusion in context of the French society in the mid-1970s. While defining it as "mentally and physically handicap, suicide people, age invalids, abused children, substance abusers, delinquents, single parents, multi problems household, marginal, asocial person and other social misfits. This concept was adopted by the European Union in the late 1980s as a key concept in social policy and in many instances replaced the concept of poverty. This concept was a response to the crisis of the welfare state and has gained foothold in the third world countries, especially India.

Some claim that social exclusion/ inclusion is more illuminating and holds the promise of understanding disadvantaged groups better, others argue that this concept is so evocative, ambiguous, multidimensional and elastic that it can be defined in different ways and owing to its ambiguity in definition it may mean all things to all people.[1]

The concept of social exclusion as it appeared in France and Europe in general was tied to the effect of the failure of integrative institution. This concept has its roots in the functionalist social theory of Emile Durkheim writing at the turn of the 20th century. Durkheim was concerned with how social order and stability could be maintained in a society where social dislocations accompanied the transitions from an agrarian to industrial society.

1.2 Social Exclusion

Social exclusion has been defined as the process through which individuals or groups are wholly or partially excluded from full participation in the society within which they live. 'An important reason for this is the fact that the concept of poverty has been difficult to define, and that it has been heavily contested whether or not this concept can fully depict the social disadvantages in today's society. One of the most popular arguments in favour of the social exclusion concept is that it takes in to account more dimensions of people's lives than the poverty concept'.[2]

Pilgram (2001) defines social exclusion as; continuous and gradual deficit of full participation in the social (including material as well as symbolic) resources produced supplied and exploited in our society for making a living, organising a life and taking part in the development of a (hopefully better) future. The concept of social exclusion has advantages over related concepts as poverty and marginalisation, since:

(i) Social exclusion is a multi-dimensional concept.

(ii) Social exclusion has a relational character. (Instead of the distributional character of the concept of poverty)

(iii) Social exclusion is a dynamic concept. (Instead of the static nature of the more traditional concepts of poverty and marginalisation)

(iv) Social exclusion is actor oriented.

(v) Social exclusion (as well as social inclusion) is closely related to the concept of participation.

(vi) Inability to participate effectively in economic, social, political, and cultural life.

(vii) Distance and alienation from a so called main stream society.

(viii) Isolation from major societal mechanisms which produce or distribute social resources.

1.3 Concept of Social Inclusion

'Inclusion' is a term that can be used to describe a series of positive actions to achieve equality of access to goods and services, to assist all individuals to participate in community and society, to encourage the contribution of all persons to social and cultural life and to be aware of and to challenge all forms of discrimination. By ensuring that the marginalised and those living in poverty have greater participation in decision-making, which affects their lives, will allow them to improve their standard of living and overall well-being.

Social inclusion is a proactive strategy to put the vulnerable groups and communities at on par with other groups that are better placed in accessing benefits. It seeks to render justice to these vulnerable groups by being fair to them in a way that they will have equal access to the opportunities, resources, services and institutions to develop themselves and be mainstreamed.

By the year 1990 the term was theorised by scholars like Bourdieu and Luhmann. The latter clarified the concept in the following terms:

The concept of inclusion means the encompassing of the entire population in the performances of the individual function systems. On the one hand this concerns access to these benefits and, on the other dependence of individual modes of living on them. To the extent that inclusion is achieved, groups disappear that do not or only marginally participate in social living.

1.4 Definition of Inclusion

Inclusion is a broad social model of adapting organisational or community facilities and processes to diversity, thus including vulnerable or oppressed groups. Social Inclusion is defined as follows:-

(1) General Definition – 'A socially inclusive society is defined as one where all people feel valued, their differences are respected, and their basic needs are met so they can live in dignity'.

(2) According to the Twelfth Five Year Plan (2012-17), 'Inclusiveness means many different things and each aspect of inclusiveness poses its own challenges for policy'.

(3) According to Luhman, "The concept of inclusion means the encompassing of the entire population in the performances of the individual function systems. On the one hand, this concerns access to these benefits and, on the other, dependence of individual modes of living on them. To the extent that inclusion is achieved, groups disappear that do not or only marginally participate in social living".

(4) The World Bank defines social inclusion as the process of improving the terms for individuals and groups to take part in society. Social inclusion aims to empower poor and marginalised people to take advantage of burgeoning global opportunities. It ensures that people have a voice in decisions which affect their lives and that they enjoy equal access to markets, services and political, social and physical spaces.

(5) An inclusive society is a society that over-rides differences of race, gender, class, generation, and geography, and ensures inclusion, equality of opportunity as well as capability of all members of the society to determine an agreed set of social institutions that govern social interaction.[3]

Inclusiveness is a process of addressing and responding to the needs of the socio-economically underprivileged sections of the society in order to bring them at par. Inclusive education is a process of addressing and responding to the socio-economically and psychologically tugged learning abilities and educational opportunities of the underprivileged sections of our society. Inclusive education incorporates the principle of access which should go to became access to quality education. And at the core of inclusive education is the right to education.

1.5 Western and Indian Understanding of Social Inclusion

All the above definitions and understanding of social exclusion and inclusion give us a clear idea of the process especially in the western context. The western context of social exclusion is primarily threaded in the context of poverty, migration, disability and the gender and racial prejudices. The post-world war II scenario brought in the realisation of a welfare state for upbringing the impoverished, migrant, uprooted, gender and racially discriminated communities and for rebuilding industrialisation and for thriving of democracy. All the socio-economic defects mentioned above could be rectified as the social and political systems in the European communities were based on equality, liberty and justice borne out of the renaissance. The European communities were amenable to social accommodation and assimilation breaking down financial, gender, social and racial barriers. In short, it was not a rigidly compartmentalised hierarchical society which was and is the case in India.

The Indian social system has inherited an exclusivist occupation-based socially stratified system rooted in the traditional Indian culture. The divine scriptures assigned functional duties to the four major caste congregations of the traditional social setup. The Brahmins learned the divine scriptures and were the messengers to god. They performed rituals for the Kshatriyas and the Vaishyas in their pursuit of salvation. The Kshatriyas ruled the kingdom and stood as protector from the enemy, while the Vaishyas indulged in commerce and trading and farming and the Shudras were assigned to menial and petty services to all the above caste congregations. The mere physical touch of the Shudras was avoided and severe social penance given for indiscretion. This highly rigid stratified social system has made social inclusion a far difficult task for the welfare state of India as compared to the European context.

The worst part of this social stratification system is that the divinely ordained Brahminical dominating attitude is inherited by all the strata of the social system, viz. the Kshatriyas, the Vaishyas and the Shudras who all look down upon the one below them. So this vicious system of top to bottom domination makes social inclusion the most difficult task humanity can undertake. So the defining difference between the western and Indian social contexts regarding social inclusion is the sheer rigid compartmentalisation of the social strata in the Indian context.

1.6 Social Context of Inclusion

We need to understand inclusion as a concept since it has been a government policy issue for last few years. Inclusion is being used alternatively for the term social justice in the last few years. Which underlines importance given for mainstreaming of the excluded.

The substance and credibility of the mainstream is an issue to be discussed later. Now inclusion of the underprivileged communities in to the mainstream is of urgent significance. Inclusion means inviting those who have been historically locked out. But the question arises as to who has the authority or right to invite others in it. It is high time to recognise and accept that all are born "in". So inclusion is recognising our universal "oneness" and "interdependence". Inclusion is recognising that you are 'one' even though we are not the same. Inclusion means fighting against exclusion and all the social diseases exclusion gives birth 'to' i.e. casteism, communalism, gender discrimination and handicapism. The fighting for inclusion involves assurance or support system to the excluded as a state policy.

Inclusion also means change and change brings anxiety and fear and social instability, so to change we need to overcome fear.

This theoretical understanding of inclusion applies to Indian social context. The Indian stratified social system has been built on rigidity and lack of dynamism, so is an extraordinary system of exclusion of the downtrodden sections of the society including women. The highlight of this stratified social system has been in the acceptance of assigned duties ordained by divine scriptures. The divine interpretation made communities accept exclusion voluntarily. The shudras and the atishudras who were the so called untouchables, worked in a pre-ordained manner to serve and clean for the upper castes.

Western colonial intervention and enlightened Indian socio-political leadership and the western liberal thought, initiated dynamism in Indian culture and especially in education system of the country. Inclusion required change and change could be brought about by raising question. To raise questions one needed to have deeper understanding and analytical acumen. This could only be brought about through education, especially education for the masses, the downtrodden and women. So education has become a necessity for social inclusiveness in society.

Education is about information, understanding, awareness, analysis, skill sets and sensitivities of social relationships. It is an empowerment, especially for the downtrodden who desire social mobility to enter the mainstream in pursuit of financial gains and new found social status.

The primary vehicle of education is the state sponsored formal education along with the private endeavour. The formal initiative has taken the form of right to education in India to cater to the children aged between 6 to 14 years. The RTE is free and compulsory with emphasis on evolutional variation, outreach to the last child private school participation, community participation and non-detention policy.

1.7 Constitutional Provisions regarding Social Welfare and Social Inclusion

The Indian Constitution guarantees all citizens basic civil and political rights and fundamental freedoms. Constitutional provisions regarding social welfare and social inclusion are as follows:

- **Right to Equality**- Constitution has provision prohibiting discrimination based on caste these provisions are found under Articles 15, 16, and 17
- **Right Against Exploitation** – Article 23
- **Cultural and Educational Rights** – Article 29:2
- **Prohibition against disenfranchisement in elections based on one's religion, race, caste or sex** – Article 325
- **Reserve seats for SC and ST in Union and state legislature** – Articles 330 and 333
- **National Commission for SC and ST** – Article 338.

Legislative Enactments

India has passed various laws to protect the rights of the Scheduled Castes to fulfill the constitutional provisions pertaining to them. These include the following:

- Protection of Civil Rights (Anti-Untouchability) Act (1955);
- The Bonded Labour (Abolition) Act (1976);
- The Scheduled Castes and Scheduled Tribes (Prevention of Atrocities) Act (1989) and Rules (1995);
- The Employment of Manual Scavenger and Construction of Dry Latrines (Prohibition) Act (1993).

Moreover, government legislated various land-reform laws to redistribute community land to the landless. Finally, to monitor enforcement of some of these laws, the Central Government established the National Commission for Scheduled Castes and Scheduled Tribes and the National Human Rights Commission in the early 1990s.

1.8 Historical Background of Inclusive Education

The history of the inclusion movement began in India with the National Policy on Education, 1968. This policy gave an emphasis on education of girls and backward groups of children it envisaged the expansion of educational facilities for children with disabilities through integration in regular schools. This policy was followed by the Integrated Education for Disabled Children Programme (MHRD, 1974) to promote education, and ensure retention of children with mild to moderate disabilities in regular schools.

(i) Inclusive Education

Inclusive education is a term commonly used to describe the process of providing access to mainstream education for children with disabilities. In this research the concept of 'Inclusive Education' used in broad view, inclusive education is an approach which seeks to address the learning needs of all children, youth and adults with a specific focus on those who are vulnerable to the marginalised and excluded. It implies that, all learners (with or without disabilities, from different categories) should learn together through common school. There is a need of inclusive education for inclusive development in the country like India where we can see the diversity and discrimination in large scale. Some definition of inclusive education are as follows:

(1) Inclusive education is the process of eliminating exclusion on the basis of social, economic and cultural background of the child in schools and other centers of learning. It is an indispensable tool to achieve social equity (UNESCO, 2009).

(2) According to the Action Plan for Inclusive Education of Children and Youth with Disabilities (MHRD, 2005)- "In its broadest and all encompassing meaning, inclusive education, as an approach, seeks to address the learning needs of all children, youth and adults with specific focus on those who are vulnerable to marginalisation and exclusion. It implies all learners, young people - with or without disabilities - being able to learn together through access to common preschool provisions, schools and community educational setting with an appropriate network of support services".

(ii) Major Reforms and Innovations for Inclusive Education

The central vision of the eleventh plan was inclusive development, to ensure broad-based improvement in the quality of life of the people especially the poor, SCs, STs, OBCs, minorities and women. This broad vision of eleventh plan includes several interrelated components– rapid growth that reduces poverty and creates employment opportunities, access to essential service in health and education especially for the poor, equality to opportunity, empowerment through education and skill development etc. Education and skill development received high priority in eleventh five year plan of India, both to meet the needs of the growing economy and to promote social equality by empowering those currently excluded because of unequal access to education and skills to participate fully in the growth process.

The tenth five year plan laid emphasis on 'Universalisation of Elementary Education' (UEE) guided by five parameters- (i) Universal access, (ii) Universal Enrolment, (iii) Universal Retention, (iv) Universal Achievement, and (v) Equity. Many innovations have been made at all level for promoting inclusive education. Some programme implemented at elementary level have been listed below:

(i) The Right of Children to free and compulsory Education (RTE), Act, 2009.

(ii) National Programme for Education of Girls at Elementary Level (NPEGEL).

(iii) Kasturba Gandhi BalikaVidyalaya (KGBV).

(iv) Mid-day Meal (MDM) Scheme.

More emphasis is now being given to those sections of the community, which are most underprivileged like girls, SC, ST, minorities children and youth with disabilities. The schemes of NPEGEL and KGBV are specifically designed for this purpose. The Mid-Day Meal scheme was initially launched as a central sponsored scheme in August 1995 to support universalisation of elementary education and to improve the nutritional status of children at primary level.

Indian government endeavoured a lot of schemes and policies to catch the goal of democratic welfare state set by the Indian Constitution. Since democracy is thrust on us, we are not trying to engage with its basic tenets, having, for centuries,functioned as a society based on traditional social values that have been completely contradictory to basic constitutional tenets. Tools of social welfare are coming out as incomplete or non-holistic responses in the process of social justice, this whole socio-psychological process leading to half-hearted efforts and ultimately to half-baked solutions.

Notes

1. Social Inclusion and Exclusion: A Review, *Dhaulagiri Journal of Sociology and Anthropology*, Oct. 2008
2. Social Inclusion and Exclusion: A Review, *Dhaulagiri Journal of Sociology and Anthropology*, Oct. 2008.
3. Expert Group Meeting "Promoting Social Integration – Convened in Preparation for the 47th session of the Commission for Social Development" Helsinki, Finland, 8-10 July 2008.

Chapter - 2

Right to Education

2.1 Introduction

India is one of the oldest civilisations of the world with traditionalism as its core character. It has been built on a social structure where social identity perpetuates the political, economic and cultural paradigms of life. India was invaded innumerable number of times but the basic structure of the society did not change much as the invaders and colonisers were not as interested in cultural invasion as they were in political domination and economic plunder. But with the colonial rule India did undergo political, social and also educational changes. We adopted democracy as a tool of self-governance. Its constitutional basic tenets of liberty, equality and justice with fraternity have helped social reforms, especially in the interests of the scheduled castes, scheduled tribes and women. But the pace of change has been tardy. But the judiciary has been proactive for socio-economic reforms and along with international convention for child rights, it forced the Indian government to come up with a path breaking act for right to education. But as discussed earlier the social system in India does not evolve perfectly in synchronisation with the political system. The political system is modernising at better pace due to a reformist leadership, enlightened with western liberal political space, based on socio-political rights and duties. The social space in India drags at a slower pace because it still believed in its inherent strength of supplementary and complimentary social castes for socio-economic and political community living, with actual identified roles for individual castes. This castes structure has been rigidly stratified and compartmentalised, disallowing any changes in roles severely limiting opportunities of social mobility for the scheduled castes, scheduled tribes along with other backward classes and women. Education or rather denial of it had been the highlight of this social structure. The upper castes had access to all education and with high productivity. But the lower castes were ordained to menial and stigmatised services for the upper castes along the centuries. This rigid structure is being shaken with radical socio-economic and political reforms through post independence legislation. The right to free and compulsory education for children between 6-14 years is one such, though having been adopted at the prompting of the judiciary. So this important right highlighting equality with opportunity for education to all including the scheduled castes and tribes is one that needs to be studied for its implementation and impact on education and to examine the overall implications for universal inclusion that is professed to be the prime objectives of the RTE act.

The right to Education has evolved after sustained international human rights pursuation and subsequent human rights declarations world over.

2.2 International Instruments

(i) Universal Declaration of Human Rights

It was adopted by general assembly. The Declaration has been hailed as an historic event of profound significance and as one of the greatest achievements of the United Nations. The Declaration "..... is the mine from which other conventions as well as national constitutions protecting these rights have been and are being quarried."

(ii) ***Preamble of the Universal Declaration of Human Rights***-Is as follows:

Whereas recognition of the inherent dignity and of the equal and inalienable rights of all members of the human family is the foundation of the freedom, justice and peace in the world. The General Assembly proclaims this Universal Declaration of Human Rights as a common standard of achievement for all people, and of all nations, to the end that every individual and every organ of society, keeping this Declaration constantly in mind, shall strive by teaching and education to promote respect of these rights and freedoms and by progressive measures, national and international, to secure their universal and effective recognition and observance, both among the peoples of Member of States themselves and among the peoples of territories under their jurisdiction.

The rights proclaimed in the Universal Declaration of Human Rights, maybe classified into following four categories:

(i) General (Articles 1 and 2),

(ii) International Covenant on Civil and Political Rights (Articles 3 to 21),

(iii) International Covenant on Economic, Social and Cultural Rights (Articles 22 to 27), and

(iv) Concluding (Articles 28 to 30) in a number of cases the judges of international court of justice have cited the provisions of universal declaration of human rights. Such as *Columbia vs. Peru, (1950), Anglo-Iranian Oil Co. Case (1955),* and *Nottebolhm Case.* The Indian Constitution also accommodates this Universal Declaration and this has been recognised by the Supreme Court of India. While referring to fundamental rights in Part-III of the Constitution *Chief Justice Sikri* observed in *Keshavanand Bharti Vs. State of Kerala* "I am unable to hold that these provisions show that some rights are not natural or inalienable rights. As a matter of fact India was a party to the Universal Declaration of Human Rights.... And that Declaration describes some fundamental rights as inalienable." The Universal Declaration which was originally conceived as a Statement of objectives to be achieved by Government and as such, no part of binding law, has now (53 years later) been accepted by so many States to be an international standard against which their behaviour is measured.

Indeed the Universal Declaration has become legally binding constituting an authoritative interpretation of the Chapter and as new rules of customary international law binding on all States. To some extent at least the Declaration has by custom recognised, as laying down rules binding upon States. The International Conference of Human Rights at Tehran has pointed out that without full realisation of economic, social and cultural rights the implementation of Civil and Political Rights was not possible. Being aware of this fact, the Commission on Human Rights expressed its deep concern in its resolution of

14 March 1985 for considerable gap prevailing in the implementation of economic, social and cultural rights in many countries of the world. In the opinion of the commission the implementation of economic, social and cultural rights has not received adequate attention within the frameworks of the United Nations system, therefore, it requested the States to direct their policy in such a manner that the realisation of social, economic and cultural rights may progressively become possible.

Economic, social and cultural rights are incorporated in the International Covenant on Economic, Social and Cultural rights which were adopted by the General Assembly on 16 December, 1966 and entered into force on 3 January. In pursuance of the general obligation undertaken by the member States under the United Nations Charter to ensure higher standard of living, full employment and conditions of economic and social progress and development, solutions of international economic, social, health, and related problems, and international cultural and educational co-operation, a number of United Nations organs are engaged in the promotional activities for realisation of economic, social and cultural rights. These various bodies, such as, the General Assembly, the Economic and Social Council, the Commission on Human Rights, the Sub-commission on Prevention of Discrimination and protection of Minorities and the Commission on Status of Women, are striving for implementation of economic, social and cultural rights. For monitoring the implementation of these rights, the Committee on Economic, Social and Cultural rights has been established. Furthermore, there are several specialised agencies of the United Nations, such as UNESCO, FAO, WHO and ILO which are engaged in the promotion of realisation of economic, social and cultural rights acting within their field of specialisation.

(iii) International Covenant on Economic, Social and Cultural Rights

The States Parties to the covenant have undertaken to take step, individually or through international economic and technical assistance and cooperation to the maximum of their available resources for achieving progressively the full realisation of rights recognised in the present covenant.

States have also guaranteed that the rights recognised in the present Covenant will be exercised without discrimination of any kind as to race, colour, sex, language, religion, political or other opinion, national or social origin, property, birth or other status. The Covenant includes the following rights: right to work; right to education; right to health; right to adequate food; right to culture; right to enjoyment of just and favourable conditions of work; right to form and join trade union; right to social security; right to family and protection of motherhood and childhood; and right to adequate standard of living.

It may be mentioned that under the International Covenant on Economic, Social and Cultural Rights the States Parties undertake "to take steps" progressively for the full realisation of the rights recognised in the present Covenant. The obligation of the States Parties under this Covenant is only "to take steps". It may be compared with their obligation under the International Covenant on Civil and Political Rights under which the States Parties undertake "to respect and ensure" to all individuals within its territory the right recognised in the said Covenant. Thus, States Parties under the International Covenant on Economic, Social and Cultural Rights are not under an obligation "to respect and ensure" to all individuals within its territory the right recognised in the said Covenant. Thus, States Parties under the International Covenant on Economic, Social and Cultural Rights are not under an obligation "to respect and ensure", rather they are under obligation "to take steps" towards the realisation of those rights incorporated therein. The position of economic, social and cultural rights is almost same as that of the Directive Principles of State Policy under the Constitution of India, for Article 37 of the Constitution provides that the provisions contained in Part IV (The Directive Principles of State Policy) shall not be enforceable by any court, rather these principles are fundamental in the governance of the country and it shall be the duty of the State to apply these principles in making laws.

(iv) The UNESCO convention against discrimination in Education

The General Conference of UNESCO had adopted the Convention against Discrimination in Education on 4 December 1996. The states parties to this convention undertake:

(a) To abrogate any statutory provision and by administrative instructions and to discontinue any administrative practices which involve discrimination in education.

(b) To ensure by legislation wherever necessary that there is no discrimination in the admission of pupils to educational institutions.

(c) Not to allow any difference of treatment by the public authorities between nationals, except on the basis of merit or need, in the matter of school fees and the grant of scholarships or other forms of assistance to pupils and necessary permits and facilities for the pursuit of studies in foreign countries.

(d) Not to allow, in any form of assistance granted by the public authorities to educational institutions, any restriction or preference based solely on the ground that pupils belong to a particular group.

(e) To give foreign nationals resident within their territory the same access to education as that given to their own nationals.

(f) To develop and apply a national policy which, by methods appropriate to the circumstances and to the national usage, will tend to promote equality of opportunity and treatment in the matter of education.

The General Conference of UNESCO had also adopted the Recommendation against Discrimination in Education on 14 December, 1960. Simultaneously with the Convention discussed above it was adopted in response to the desire to take account of the difficulties which certain states might, because of their federal structure, experience in ratifying the Convention. The provisions of the Recommendation are identical with that of the Convention.

The General Conference of UNESCO also adopted in 10 December, 1962, the protocol instituting a Conciliation and Good offices Commission with the responsibility to settle any dispute which may arise between the State Parties to the convention against discrimination in education.[1]

2.3 Historical Evolution of RTE in India

The path of the Right to Education in India was not simple and easy. For the understanding of the obstacles in the Universalisation of education in India, we have to review the ancient education system of India. Education in ancient India has been notorious for not being socially inclusive. Till the 19th century, it was largely considered a privilege restricted to persons at the higher end of the caste or class system. 'In the Vedic period, education was the sole privilege of the priestly Dwija castes. People from lower castes, and so called 'shudras' (Untouchables), in particular, were barred from receiving education. In the medieval period, the Muslim rulers of India also did not consider education as a function of the state. It was perceived as a branch of religion and therefore entrusted to learned theologians called 'Ulemas'. Therefore, in ancient and medieval India, education was interlocked with religion and was clearly not accessible to all persons.'[2]

Buddhism and Jainism overthrew the dominance of classical Vedic Education by the end of the eighth century AD, freeing education beyond the confines of hermitages. Education was open to all castes and women also.

In the colonial period, the British rulers introduced new modern education system in India. This education system was not a spontaneous benevolent act of the British administrators, but it was to serve their vested interests. The British rulers wanted clerks, managers for the political administration in India. However, the untouchables got education in the colonial period, which were neglected in the ancient education system.

(i) Pre-independence - Efforts for Right to Education

'Prior to the right to education in India, interestingly there was provision for compulsory education acts pre and post independence throughout the provinces of the British India in response to pursuit by Indian leaders and princely state such as Baroda. These attempts began about a century ago under the European influence with emergence of ideas of 'native state' and its social welfare manifestation. With these ideas merge new concepts regarding education as a right to citizen and as duty of the state. In the later half of the 19th century the visits of Indian leadership to Europe exposed to them to the difference in the entitlement of citizens in England and in British India.'

In 1870, England passed legislation to make education free and compulsory leading to a similar demand in India. Educated Indians deposed before the Indian education commission in 1882 and asked for compulsory education and wean away children from labour in factories.

The princely states of Baroda, Travancare, Manipur introduced legislation in their states to make education compulsory to prove to the British that the idea of education for all was not impossible.

A overview of the major historical milestones regarding compulsory education in India:

1870-80 Compulsory Education Act passed in Britain- Demand for similar treatment for Indians.

1882 Indian Education Commission-Indian leaders demand provision for mass Education and Compulsory Education Acts.

1893 Maharaja of Baroda introduces Compulsory Education for Boys in Amreli Taluk.

1906 Maharaja of Baroda extends Compulsory Education to rest of the state.

1906 Gopal Krishna Gokhale makes a plea to Imperial Legislative Council for introduction of Free and Compulsory Education.

1911 Gokhale proposes Private members Bill (Rejected).

1917 Shri. Vithalbhai Patel succeeds in getting Bill passed.

1917 First Law on Compulsory Education passed (Popularly Known as Patel Act).

1918-1930 Every Province in British India gets Compulsory Education Act on its Statute Book.

1930 Hartog Committee Recommendation for better quality (not quantity) hinders spread and development of primary education.

1944 Post-war plan for Education development in India (Sargent plan) proposes scheme for India to achieve universal elementary education by 1948 (40 years).

1947 Ways and Means (Kher) Committee set up to explore ways and means of achieving UEE within ten years at lesser cost.

1947 Constituent Assembly sub-committee on fundamental rights places free and compulsory education on list of fundamental rights.

Clause 23- Every citizen is entitled as of right to free primary education and it shall be the duty of the state to provide within a period of ten years from the commencement of this constitution for free and compulsory education for all children until they complete the age of fourteen years.

1947 (Apr.) Advisory committee of the constituent assembly rejects free and compulsory education as a fundamental right. Sends clause to list of non-justifiable fundamental rights (later termed as Directive Principles of State Policy).

1949 (Nov.) Debate in constituent assembly removes the first line of this clause (now Article 36) i.e. "Every citizen is entitled as of right to free primary education and it shall be the duty of the state to….. "and replaces it with The state shall endeavour to…." and Dr B.R. Ambedkar, clarifies that the objective of Article 36 is not restricted to free primary education. ..."The clause as it stands after the amendment is that every child shall be kept in an educational institution under training until the child is of 14 year"....... "a provision is made in Article 18 to forbid any child being employed below the age of 14. Obviously, if the child is not to be employed below the age of 14, the child must be kept occupied in some educational institution. That is the object of Article 36, and that is why I say the world "primary" is quite inappropriate."

1950 Article 45 of the Directive Principles of State Policy of the newly adopted constitution of India, provides that: "The State shall endeavour to provide, within a period of ten years from the commencement of this constitution, for free and compulsory education for all children until they complete the age of fourteen years."[3]

The right to education issue has been debated in India for more than a century. A substantial part of the memorandum, presented by Mahatma Jyotiba Phule to the Indian Education Commission in 1882, dwelt upon how the British government's funding of education tended to benefit Brahmins and higher classes while leaving "the masses wallowing in ignorance and poverty". 'In the evidence placed before the Hunter Commission appointed in 1882, Dadabhai Naoroji and Jyotiba Phule from Bombay demanded state sponsored free education for at least four years. This demand was indirectly acknowledged in the commission's recommendations on primary education. The Commission recommended that schools should be open to all castes and classes. In the first decade of 20th century Sir Chimanlal Shitalwad and Sir Ibrahim Rahimatulla strongly demanded the provincial government to make education compulsory in the Bombay city. In order to pacify them an advisory committee on this issue was appointed in 1906. The committee declared forcefully that it was rather before time and hence impossible to start compulsory education in Bombay. On the contrary, Maharaja Sayajirao Gaikwad made this impossible thing possible by initiating compulsory primary education in 9 villages of Amroli district in his State of Baroda as a pre-test in the year 1893 AD. After getting positive results, State of Baroda was first to introduce law on Compulsory Education in 1906. This law provided for compulsory education for boys and girls in the age groups of 7 to 12 years and 7-10 years respectively. The first documented use of the word right in the context of elementary education appears in a letter written by Rabindranath Tagore to the International League for the Rational Education of Children in 1908AD.'[4]

Another attempt to get elementary education recognised as a right was made, though obliquely, way back in 1909 when G. K. Ghokhale introduced a Bill under the Indian Council Act of 1909, to make primary education compulsory, and deserving of State funding. However, the Bill was defeated by a large majority. While addressing the legislatures, Ghokhale made the emotional observation that the issue would keep coming up again and again until all children realised their right to free and compulsory education.

'In 1937, at the National Education Conference held at Wardha, Mahatma Gandhi had to use all the moral powers at his command to persuade the Ministers of Education of the newly elected Congress governments to implement free and compulsory education of seven years and allocate adequate funds for this purpose. In spite of this, the Wardha Conference passed four resolutions among which the first one stated that in the opinion of this Conference, free and compulsory education is provided for seven years on a nation-wide scale. This resolution on free and compulsory education was re-iterated by the 51st annual session of Indian National Congress held at Haripura in February 1938.'[5]

'The next landmark development in the history of free and compulsory education in India was the post war plan of education development of 1944, also called the Sargent Plan, which recommended free and compulsory education for eight years (6-14 years age group)'[6]

Despite the consistent demand for free and compulsory education during the freedom struggle, at the time of drafting the Constitution, there was no unanimous view that the citizens of India should have a right to education, let alone a fundamental right. The Constitution Assembly Debates reveal that an amendment was moved to alter the draft Article relating to free and compulsory education, by removing the term entitled to ensure that it was merely a non-justifiable policy directive in the Constitution. Therefore, free and compulsory education made its way into the Constitution as a directive principle of State Policy under the Article 45, whereby States were required to ensure that free and compulsory education was provided to all children till the age of fourteen.

The effects of above-mentioned initiatives had come in forms of various committees and national policies on education after independence.

(ii) Legislation for Compulsory Education in India

This long history of legislation on compulsory education in pre and post independent India serves to emphasise the point that legislation alone cannot bring about universalisation of elementary education as proved by the fact we harbour the largest number of illiterates in the world. The list of compulsory education acts in pre and post independent India is as follows:

1. The Bombay Primary Education (District Municipalities) Act, 1917
2. The Bengal Primary Education Act, 1919
3. The Bihar and Orissa Primary Education Act, 1919
4. The Punjab Compulsory Education Act, 1919
5. The United Provinces Primary Education Act, 1919
6. The Bombay City Primary Education Act, 1920
7. The Central Provinces Primary Education Act, 1920
8. The Madras Primary Education Act, 1920
9. The Patiala primary Education Act, 1926

10. The Bikaner State Compulsory Primary Education Act, 1922
11. The Madras Primary Education Act, 1937.
12. The Bombay City Primary Education (District Boards) Act, 1922
13. The Bombay Primary Education Act, 1923
14. The Assam Primary Education Act, 1936
15. The U.P.(District Boards) Primary Education Act, 1926
16. The Bengal (Rural) Primary Education Act, 1930
17. The (Jammu & Kashmir) Compulsory Education Act, 1934
18. The Bombay Primary Education (Amendment) Act, 1938
19. The Punjab Primary Education Act, 1940
20. The Mysore Elementary Education Act, 1941
21. The Travancore Primary Education Act, 1945
22. The Bombay Primary Education Act, 1947

(iii) Post Independent

1. The Assam Primary Education Act, 1947
2. The Bombay Primary Education Act, 1947
3. The Cochin Free Compulsory Primary Education Act, 1947
4. The Madhya Pradesh Compulsory Primary Education Act, 1950
5. The Ajmer Primary Education Act, 1952
6. The Madras Elementary Education Act, 1952
7. The Hyderabad Compulsory Primary Education Act, 1952
8. The Vindhya Pradesh Primary Education Act 1952
9. The Himachal Pradesh Compulsory Primary Education Act, 1953
10. The Assam Basic Education Act, 1954
11. The PEPSU Compulsory Primary Education Act, 1956
12. The Bhopal State Compulsory Primary Act, 1956
13. The Madhya Pradesh Primary Education Act, 1956
14. The Saurashtra Primary Education Education Act, 1956
15. The Kerala Education Act, 1958
16. The Delhi Primary Education Act, 1960
17. The Andhra Pradesh Primary Education Act, 1961

18. The Andaman and Nicobar Islands (Primary Education) Regulation, 1959
19. The Assam Elementary Education Act, 1962

The efforts and the constitutional provision for the free and compulsory elementary education after independence are as follows:

(iv) Post-independent Right to Education

In 1950, India adopted its own Constitution, which provided fundamental rights to equality, to freedom, against exploitation, to freedom of religion, to constitutional remedies and cultural and educational rights of the minorities. The Indian Constitution recognised the need of free and compulsory education as well.

(v) Constitutional Provisions Protecting the Right of the Child

In the Indian Constitution, Articles 24 and 39 dealing with prohibition of children from being employed in factories, mines or in other hazardous employment; development and protection of the tender age of children; and free and compulsory education.

As per **Article 24** of the Indian Constitution, no child below the age of 14 years shall be employed to work in any factory or mine or engaged in hazardous employment.

As per **Article 39** of the Indian Constitution, the state shall direct its policy toward securing that the tender age of children is not abused and that citizens are not forced by economic necessity to enter avocation unsuited to their age or strength and that children are given opportunities and facilities to develop in a healthy manner and in conditions of freedom and dignity and that childhood and youth are protected against exploitation and against moral and material abandonment.

'**Article 29 and 30** of the Indian constitution provide citizens the Educational and Cultural Rights. Similarly, Directives of the state policy emphasized on intellectual development of the Citizens'[7] Article 41 of the Constitution lays down that the state shall, within the limits of its economic capacity and development, make effective provision for securing the right to education.

'**Article 45 of part IV** of the Constitution declared, that the state shall endeavor to provide, within a period of ten years from the commencement of this Constitution, for free and compulsory education for all children until they complete the age of fourteen years.'[8] This policy directed to provide free and compulsory education to the children below the age of 14 in the suggested timeframe. However, for the rapid development after independence Indian government emphasized on the economic development and gave priority to investment in higher and technical education.

Article 46 of the Constitution states that, "The state shall promote, with special care, the education and economic interests of the weaker sections of the people, and particular of the Scheduled Castes and Scheduled Tribes, and shall protect them from social exploitation." Articles 330, 332, 335, 338 to 342 and entire Fifth and Sixth schedules of the Constitution deal with the special provisions for implementation of the objectives set forth in Article 46. These provisions need to be fully utilised for the benefit of the weaker sections of our society.

(vi) Judicial Pronouncements on RTE

'Right to Education has been recognised as a human right to be protected and preserved. Its importance has also been recognised by the framers of the Constitution under 44 of the Constitution. So as to convert a Right to Education into a fundamental right to education the courts in India played a vital role'.

Mohini Jain Vs. State of Karnataka and others: The observations of the court are as follows:

The directive principles which are fundamental in the governance of the country cannot be isolated from the fundamental rights guaranteed under Part III. These principles have to be read into the fundamental rights. Both are supplementary to each other. The State is under a constitutional mandate to create conditions in which the fundamental rights guaranteed to the individuals under Part III could be enjoyed by all. Without making "right to education" under Article 41 of the Constitution a reality the fundamental rights under Chapter III shall remain beyond the reach of large majority which is illiterate.

"Right to life" is the compendious expression for all those rights which the Courts must enforce because they are basic to the dignified enjoyment of life. It extends to the full range of conduct which the individual is free to pursue. The right to education flows directly from right to life. The right to life under article 21 and the dignity of an individual cannot be assured unless it is accompanied by the right to education. The State Government is under an obligation to make endeavor to provide educational facilities at all levels to its citizens.

The fundamental rights guaranteed under Part III of the Constitution of India including the right to freedom of speech and expression and other rights under Article 19 cannot be appreciated and fully enjoyed unless a citizen is educated and is conscious of his individualistic dignity.

The "right to education", therefore, is concomitant to the fundamental rights enshrined under Part III of the Constitution. The state is under a constitutional-mandate to provide educational institution at all levels for the benefit of the citizens. The educational institutions must function to the best advantage of the citizens. Opportunity to acquire education cannot be confined to the richer section of the society.

The Court holds that every citizen has a 'right to education' under the Constitution. The state is under an obligation to establish educational institutions to enable the citizens to enjoy the said right. The state may discharge its obligation through State-owned or State-recognised educational institutions. When the State Government grants recognition to the private educational institutions it creates an agency to fulfill its obligation under the Constitution. The students are given admission to the educational institutions whether State-owned or State-recognised in recognition of their 'right to education' under the Constitution. Charging capitation fee in consideration of admission to educational institutions, is a patent to educational institutions, is a patent denial of a citizen's right to education under the Constitution.

Indian civilisation recognises education as one of the pious obligations of the human society. To establish and administer educational institutions is considered a religious and charitable object. Education in India has never been a commodity for sale. Looking at the economic-front, even seventy-four years after achieving independence, thirty percent of the population is living below poverty line and the bulk of the remaining population is struggling for existence under poverty-conditions. The preamble promises and the directive principles are a mandate to the State to eradicate poverty so the poor of this country can enjoy the right to life guaranteed under the Constitution. The State action or inaction per se arbitrary and cannot be sustained. Capitation fee makes the availability of education beyond the reach of the poor.

Unnikrishnan, JP and others Vs. State of Andhara Pradesh and others

The Court observes right to education a fundamental right or not... In order to treat a right as a fundamental right it is not necessary that it should be expressly stated as one in Part III of the Constitution. The provisions of Part III and IV are supplementary and complementary to each other. Fundamental rights are but a means to achieve the goal indicated in Part IV and must be constructed in the light of the directive principles.

Though right to education is not stated expressly as a fundamental right, it is implicit in and flows from the right to life guaranteed under Article 21 having regard to the broad and expansive interpretation given by the Court. The right to education has been treated as one of transcendental importance. It has fundamental significance to the life of an individual and the nation. Without education being provided to the citizens of this country, the objectives set forth in the Preamble to the Constitution cannot be achieved. The Constitution would fail.

The fact that right to education occurs in as many as three Articles in Part IV *viz.,* Articles 41, 45 and 46 shows the importance attached to it by the founding fathers. Even some of the Articles in Part III *viz..,* Articles 29 and 30 speak of education.

That right to education is implicit in the right to life so that the State cannot deprive the citizen of his right to education except in accordance with the procedure prescribed by law. The right to education which is implicit in the right to life and personal liberty guaranteed by Article 21 must be constructed in the light of the directive principles in Part IV of the Constitution.

Right to education, understood in the context of Articles 45 and 41 means: (a) every child/citizen of this country had a right to free education until he completes the age of fourteen years and (b) after a child/citizen completes 14 years, his right to education is circumscribed by the limits of the economic capacity of the State and its development.

The right to education which flows from Article 21 is not an absolute right. It must be constructed in the light of directive principles.

A true democracy is one where education is universal, where people understand what is good for them and the nation and knows how to govern them. Articles 45, 46 and 41 are designed to achieve the said goal among others. It is in the light of these articles that the content and parameters of the right to education have to be determined. Right to education, understood in the context of Articles 45 and 41, means that every child/citizen of this country has a right to free education until he completes the age of fourteen years and (b) after a child/citizen completes 14 years, his right to education is circumscribed by the limits of the economic capacity of the State and its development. It is significant that among the several articles in Part IV, only Article 45 speaks of a time-limit; no other article does. It is not a mere pious wish and the State cannot flout the said direction even after 62 years on the ground that the article merely calls upon it to "Endeavour to provide" the same and on the further ground that the said article is not enforceable by virtue of the declaration in Article 37. The passage of 62 years –more than four times the period stipulated in Article 45 – has converted the obligation created by the article into an enforceable right. At least now the State should honour the command of Article 45. It must be made a reality.

This does not however mean that this obligation can be performed only through the State schools. It can be also be done by permitting, recognising and aiding voluntary non-governmental organisations, who are prepared to impart free education to children. This does not also mean that unaided private schools cannot continue. They indeed can, they too have a role to play. They meet the demand of that segment of population who may not wish to have their children educated in State-run schools. They have necessarily to charge fees from the students.

While allocating the available resources, due regard should be given to the wise words of Founding Fathers in Articles 45 and 46. Though the importance and significance of higher education cannot be denied, but there should be a proper balancing of the various sectors of education.

The right to free education is available only to children until they complete the age of 14 years. Thereafter, the obligation of the State to provide education is subject to the limits of its economic capacity and development of the State. A citizen has a right to call upon the

State to provide educational facilities to him within the limits of its economic capacity and development. The limits of economic capacity are ordinary speaking, matters within the subjective satisfaction of the State. The obligations created by Articles 41, 45 and 46 of the Constitution can be discharged by the State either by establishing institutions of its own or by aiding, recognising and/or granting affiliation to private educational institutions. Private educational institutions are a necessity in the present day context. It is not possible to do without them because the Governments are in no position to meet the demand- particularly in the sector of medical and technical education which call for substantial outlays. While education is one of the most important functions of the Indian State it has no monopoly therein. Private educational institutions - including minority educational institutions – too have a role to play.

Anilkumar Roy Sharma Vs. State:-The Court observed "The rights of a student below fourteen years to appear in class VIII board are a facet of right to education guaranteed under Article 21 of the Constitution.

In the case of *Bandhuwa Mukti Morcha* vs. *Union of India and others* it has been held that it is the solemn duty of the state to provide basic education to children also working in different industries or factories and the court directed the government to take such steps and evolve scheme assuring education to all children either by the industry itself or in co-ordination with it.

In the case of *TMA Pai Foundation* vs. *State of Karnataka* the scheme formulated by the court in the case of Unni Krishnan was held to be an unreasonable restriction within the meaning of Article 19(6) of the Constitution as it resulted in revenue shortfalls making it difficult for the educational institutions. Consequently, all orders and directions issued by the state in furtherance of the directions in Unni Krishnan's case was held to be unconstitutional. The court observed that right to establish and administer an institution includes the right to admit students; rights to set up a reasonable fee structure; right to constitute a governing body; right to appoint staff and right to take disciplinary action.

Frankly speaking, TMA Pai foundation's case for the first time brought into existence the concept of education as an 'occupation', a term used in Article 19(1)(g) of the Constitution. The majority held that Article 19(1) (g) and Article 26 confer rights on all citizens and religious denominations respectively to establish and maintain educational institutions. Additionally, Article 30(1) gives the right to religious and linguistic minorities to establish and administer educational institution of their choice.

In *Islamic Academy of Education* vs. *State of Karnataka*, another issue arose for the determination of fees structure in private unaided professional educational institutions. It was submitted that management has been given complete autonomy not only as regard to admission of students but also as regards to fee structure which could include a reasonable revenue surplus for the purpose of development of education and expansion of education. The Apex Court also held that right of education further means that a citizen has a right to call upon the state to provide educational facilities within the limits of its economic capacity and development.

In connection to this, the Supreme Court in the case of *State of Bihar and others* vs. *Project Uchcha Vidhya, Sikshak Sangh and others* vs. *Union of India*, also observed that establishment of High Schools may not be a constitutional function in the sense that citizens of India above 14 years might not have any fundamental right in relation thereto, but education as a part of human development indisputably is a human right. Chief Justice of India Dr A.K. Lakshmanan rightly observed:

"(E)ducation is perhaps the most important function of state and a local government. It is required in the performance of our most basic responsibilities, even service in the armed forces. It is the very foundation of good citizenship. Today, it is the principal instrument in awakening the child to cultural values, in preparing him for later professional training, and in helping him to adjust normally to his environment. In these days, it is doubtful whether a child can be expected to succeed in life if he is denied the opportunity of education."

The similar kind of observations regarding fundamental significance of education has also been made by Justice S.B. Sinha in the case of *Election Commission of India* vs. *Saint Merry's School & Others*.[9]

2.4 Policies and Committees on Education

After independence as per demand of free education and other, the Indian Government set up various committees and policies on education.

(i) Kothari Commission (1964)

The Kothari Commission (1964-66) was last commission set up on education. As regards school education, the highlights of the report, submitted in 1966, advocated, inter alia (i) improving the system in existence, (ii) setting up State Boards of Education, (iii) leveling of institutions for equality, (iv) setting up area-specific neighbourhood schools, (v) establishment of Common School and (vi) a statutory School Education Commission.

This commission gives much importance to Common School system because they said that the common school system will eradicate many problems and give common platform to every individual.

(ii) The National Policy on Education (1968)

Based on the report and recommendations of the Kothari Commission (1964-66) the government of India announced first national policy on education in India 1968. This Policy called for a "radical restructuring" and equalised educational opportunities in order to achieve national integration and greater cultural and economic development. The policy called for fulfilling compulsory education for all children up to the age of 14, as stipulated by the Constitution of India, and the better training and qualification of teachers.

(iii) The National Policy For Children (1974)

The National Policy for Children, 1974 considered that to ensure the equality of opportunity to all children there is need of various child development programmes. This policy provides the framework for various needs of children, and how it responds to them in an integrated manner. Other policies, programmes, and schemes for child development have been formulated based on this National Policy. Another important aims of this policy was to infer the new provisions to Constitution for the all round development (physical, mental and social development) of the children.

The policy has suggested drawing up the programme with the available resources to provide the free and compulsory education for all children up to the age of fourteen.

(iv) National Policy on Education (1986)

The National Policy on Education (NPE) was announced in 1986. This policy called for "special emphasis on the removal of disparities and to equalise educational opportunity," especially for Indian women, Scheduled Tribes (ST) and the Scheduled Castes (SC) communities. To achieve these, the policy called for expanding scholarships, adult education, recruiting more teachers from the SCs, incentives for poor families to send their children to school regularly, development of new institutions, and providing housing and services. The NPE, (1986) called for a "child-centered approach" in primary education, and launched "Operation Blackboard" to improve primary schools nationwide.

(v) National Policy on Education (1992)

National Policy on Education 1986, while reaffirming the goal of Universalisation of elementary education, did not recognise the 'Right to Education'. This policy was reviewed by the Acharya Rammurti Committee in 1990, and this review process contributed to the revised National Policy on Education of 1992. The Acharya Rammurti Committee recommended the right to education should be included as a fundamental right in part III of the constitution. However, this recommendation was not implemented immediately.

2.5 History of Right to Education/Timeline of important events after independence[10]

- **1950**: Constitution of India contained Article 45, as one of the directive principles of State policy, which states that:

  "The State shall endeavour to provide within a period of ten years from the commencement of this Constitution, for free and compulsory education for all children until they complete the age of fourteen years."

- **1968**: First National Commission for education under Dr Kothari submits its reports. It introduced several far-reaching changes as uniform curriculum for both, the boys and girls, mathematics and science as compulsory subjects etc. It also proposed a Common School System.

- **1976**: Constitution amendment making education a concurrent subject (responsibility of both state and center) was passed.
- **1986**: National Policy on Education (NPE) endorsing Common School System (CSS) was formulated. Subsequent NPE's endorsed CSS but it has never been implemented.
- **1993**: The Supreme Court in the case of *Unnikrishnan vs State of Andhra Pradesh* ruled that the right to education is a fundamental right that flows from the Right to Life in Article 21 of the Constitution.
- **1997**: Constitution Amendment making Education a fundamental right was introduced.
- **2002**: 86th Constitution Amendment added Article 21A stating that "The State shall provide free and compulsory education to all children of the age six to fourteen years in such as a way as the State may, by law, determine." The 86th Amendment also modified Article 45 which reads as "The state shall endeavour to provide early childhood care and education for all children until they complete the age of 6 years".
- **2005**: CABE committee report constituted to draft the Right to Education Bill submits its report.
- **July 2006**: Media reports indicate that federal government is planning to ask all state governments to pass Right to Education bill in their respective legislatures based on a model bill drafted by federal Government. It has shelved plans to introduce a federal bill in this regard.

As the effects of all above mentioned commission and policies and efforts from the educationist and activist and social reformers the Indian Parliament passed the 86th amendment of constitution which added a new clause in Article 21 and created new clause, Article 21-A in the year of 2002 which made Right to Education a fundamental right. Subsequently, "Right to Free and Compulsory Education Act" was approved by the president of India on 26th August 2009 and got officially published in the gazette of India on 27th August 2009. India became one of the 135 countries to make education a fundamental right for its citizens when the act came into force on 1st April, 2010.

2.6 Main Features of the RTE Act

1. Every child of India in the 6 to 14 years age group has a right to free and compulsory education in a neighbourhood school till the completion of elementary education.
2. Children who have either dropped out from the school or have not attended any school will be enrolled in the schools and no school can deny them for taking admission.
3. Private and unaided educational institutes will have to reserve 25 percent of the seats for the students belonging to economically weaker section and disadvantaged section of the society in admission to class first (to be reimbursed by the state as part of the public-private partnership plan).
4. All schools except government schools are required to be recognised by meeting the specified norms and standards within 3 years, failing of which they will be penalised for up to Rs. one lakh. It also prohibits all unrecognised schools from practice and makes provisions for no donation or capitation fees and no interview of the child or parent at the time of admission.
5. For the purpose of admission in a school, the age of a child shall be determined on the basis of certificate issued in accordance with the provisions of the Births, Deaths and marriages Registration Act, 1856 or on the basis of such other document, as may be prescribed.
6. The National Commission for Protection of Child Rights (NCPCR) and state commissions will monitor the implementation of the Act.
7. All schools except private unaided schools are to be managed by school managing committees with 75 percent parents and guardians as members.
8. Child's mother tongue as medium of instruction, and comprehensive and continuous evaluation system of child's performance will be employed.
9. Financial burdens will be shared by the centre and the state governments in the ratio of 55:45 and this ratio is 90:10 for the north-eastern states.

2.7 Highlighting characteristics of Right Based elementary education of selective countries

Much before the implementation of the right to education in India the basic education right has been implemented in the developed, developing and even some third world countries. To understand the comparative inclusive nature of the basic characteristics of the right to education of these countries we hereby try to understand the primary provisions of their acts that further the all-round development of their children for the bright future of the nation.

Basic Education Act 68/1998 of Finland

Section- 1: Application

(i) Provides for basic education and compulsory schooling.

(ii) In addition, it provides pre-primary education, which is a year preceding compulsory schooling, voluntary additional basic education for those who have completed the basic education syllabus for instruction preparing immigrants for basic education and for before and after school activities.

(iii) Also provided for persons other than those of compulsory school age.

Section-2: Objective of Education

(i) The purpose of education referred to in this Act is to support pupils' growth in to humanity and in to ethically responsible membership of society and to provide them with knowledge and skills needed in life. Furthermore, the aim of pre-primary education, as part of early childhood education, is to improve children's capacity for learning.

(ii) Education shall promote civilisation and equality in society and otherwise developing themselves during their lives.

(iii) The aim of education shall further be to secure adequate equity in education throughout the country.

Section-3: The Foundation for Education

(i) Education shall be provided according to the pupil's age and capabilities and so as to promote healthy growth and development in the pupils.

Section-4: Statutory duty to arrange basic education and pre-primary education

(i) Local authority shall have on obligation to arrange basic education for children of compulsory school age residing in its area and pre- primary education during the year preceding compulsory schooling along with arrangement of pre-primary education for children within prolonged compulsory schooling and also children who start their basic education one year later.

(ii) Local authority in whose area a hospital is located shall be responsible for arranging teaching to a pupil who is a patient to the extent that his/ her health and circumstances allow.

(iii) Local authority in the Municipality which has both Finnish and Swedish speaking residents shall be responsible for arranging basic and pre-primary education separately for both linguistic groups.

Section-6: The determination of pupil school

(i) Education shall be arranged in municipality so as to make pupils travel to and from school as safe and short as possible in view of the habitation, the location of schools and other places of education and public transportation. In the arrangement of pre-primary education account shall additionally be taken of the participating children's access to daycare services.

(ii) Local authority shall assign to a child of compulsory school age and other receiving education under this act a neighbourhood school.

(Procedural obstacles for children and their parents for approaching neighbourhood school for admission is the neighbourhood school completely avoided is the Finnish system)

(iii) A child may not, without the consent of the parent/ carer be assigned to education for which a fee is charged.

Section-7: Register Association or foundation as education provider

(a) The government may authorise a register association or foundation to provide education conditional on a specific educational or a cultural need for the provision on an agreement between the education provider and the local authority in whose area the education is provided.

Section-9: Duration of education

(i) Nine year.

(ii) Pre-Primary education and voluntary additional education shall be one year in duration. The duration of pre-primary education in special needs education given to pupils within prolonged compulsory schooling under section 10 (4) shall be two years.

(iii) The extent of instruction preparing immigrants for basic education shall correspond to a one year syllabus.

Section-10: Language of Instruction

(i) Finnish or Swedish and native languages such as Raami, Roma or sign languages.

(ii) Additionally, in a separate teaching groups or in a separate school, teaching may be given primarily or totally in a language other than those preferred above.

Section- 11: Content of Education

(i) The basic education syllabus shall contain, as enacted by virtue of section 14, the following core subjects. Mother tongue and literature languages, environmental studies, health education, religious education or ethics, history, social studies, mathematics, physics, chemistry, biology, geography, physical education, music, art, crafts and home economics. Education may as enacted by virtue of section 14, be based on syllabi of different extent. Providers of basic education who have been assigned a special educational mission under section 7 or 8 may deviate from the provisions of this subsection.

Section- 14: Allocation of lesson hours and core curriculum

(i) The National Board of Education shall determine the objectives and core contents of different subject and cross-curriculum themes, guidance counseling and other education referred to in this act and the basic principles of home school cooperation and pupil welfare under the purview of the local education authority.

Section-16: Remedial teaching and part time special needs education

(i) A pupil who has temporarily fallen in studies or otherwise need short-term support in learning shall be entitled to remedial teaching.

(ii) A pupil who has difficulties in learning or in schooling shall be entitled to part time special needs education.

Section 16 A: Enhanced Support

(i) A pupil who needs regular support in learning or school going shall be provided enhanced support in accordance with a learning plan devised for him or her.

Section 17- Special Needs Support

(i) Special Need Support consist of special needs education and other support provided under this Act. Special-need education is provided, allowing for the pupils interests and the facilities for providing the education in conjunction with other instruction or partly or totally in a special-needs classroom or some other appropriate facility.

Section 17A: Plan on individual teaching arrangements

(i) A view to executing a decision on special need support, a plan on individual teaching arrangements shall be devised for the pupil.

Section 18: Special teaching arrangements

(1) A pupils education may to a certain degree be arranged otherwise than provided in this Act if:

(i) The pupil is considered to have some degree of prior knowledge and skills corresponding to the basic education syllabus.

(ii) The completion of the basic education syllabus would in some respect be unreasonable for the pupil in view of the circumstances and prior learning.

(iii) It is justified for reasons relating to the pupils health.

Section 21: Educational Evaluation

(i) The purpose of the evaluation of education is to assure that the purpose of this act is carried out, to support educational development and to improve conditions for learning.

(ii) An education provider shall evaluate the education it provides and its impact and take part in external evaluation of its opposition.

Section 22: Pupil Assessment

(i) The aim of pupil assessment is to guide and encourage learning and to develop the pupil capability for self assessment. The pupils learning work and behaviour shall be variously assessed.

(ii) The assessment of learning attainment and progress in studies shall be governed by the provision enacted by decree and regulation issued by the national board of education.

(iii) Unless of pupils parent or carer has proposed that the pupil repeat the year or class because of the pupils overall school attainment, the parent/ carer shall be given an opportunity to be heard before decision is made in the matter.

Section 23: School year

(a) 190 School days

Section 24: Pupils Workload

(i) The pupil's workload in basic education must be such as to allow him/ her enough time for rest, recreation and hobbies over and above time spent in school, school travel and homework.

Section 25: Compulsory Education

(i) All residing in Finland

(ii) Starting at 7 years

(iii) For ten year or shall end when the basic education syllabus has been completed.

(iv) If owing to the child disabilities or illness, the objective set for basic education cannot be achieved in nine year; compulsory schooling shall begin one year earlier than provided and for 11 years.

Section 26: Completion of compulsory schooling

(i) If a child of compulsory school age does not participate in education provided under this act, the local authority of the pupil's place of residence shall supervise his/ her progress.

Section 26A: Right to pre-primary education

(i) The child shall be entitled to pre-primary education during the year preceding of the beginning the year of compulsory schooling

Section 28. Place of schooling

(i) The child of compulsory school age may also apply for place in a school other than one referred by the local authority. However, the local authority may decide to give precedence to children residing in its area in admission to education provided by it.

Section 29: Right to safe learning environment

(i) A pupil is entitled to safe learning environment. The education provider shall draw up a plan, in connection with curriculum design, safeguarding pupils against violence, bullying and harassment, execute the plan and supervise adherence and its implementation.

Section 31: Free Education

(i) Teaching the necessary textbooks and other learning material and school equipment and material shall be free of charge for the pupil. A disabled child or a child with SENs has additionally the right to get the interpretation and assistance service he/ she needs to participate in education, other education service, special aids and the service provider under special needs education free of charge to pupil attending a basic education shall be provided with a balance and appropriately organised and supervised meal on every school day.

Section 31 A: Pupil Welfare

(i) A pupil shall be entitled the free pupil welfare necessary for participation in education. Pupil welfare means action promoting and maintaining good learning, good mental and physical health and social well-being and condition to these. (P. W.)

(ii) Pupil welfare shall encompass pupil welfare determined in the curriculum adopted by the education provider and pupil welfare services comprising school healthcare and support to school going.

Section 32: School Travel

(i) Free transport for pupils residing beyond 5 km.

(ii) For pre-primary student also free.

(iii) If travel is too difficult or dangerous there is also free transport.

(iv) Daily travel time should not exceed two and half-hours.

Section 33: Accommodation

(i) If the school travels of the pupil in the basic education, in additional education or pre-primary education for those within prolonged compulsory schooling cannot be arranged in a manner referred in above section. The pupil shall be entitled to free accommodation and boarding.

(ii) During the school year, the pupil shall be entitled to free travel between the place of accommodation as his/ her home during holiday and weekends.

Section 34: Treatment of an Accident and Healthcare

(i) An injury due to an accident and which takes place at school or in some other place of teaching, during school travel and in accommodation shall be treated free of charge for the pupil.

Section 36: Discipline

(i) A pupil transgresses against school order or cheats may be kept in detention for a maximum of two hours or may be given a written warning.

(ii) A pupil who disrupts teaching may be dismissed from the class room or other teaching facility for the remainder of the class or be ordered to leave a school function.

Section 36A: Procedure in a discipline matter and enforcement of suspension

(i) The pupil must be heard with necessary investigation before disciplinary action.

(ii) The education provider arranges teaching to prevent a suspended pupil from falling behind the progress made by his/ her year class or teaching group. A personal plan should be devised for the same.

Section 45: Dereliction of supervisory Duties

(i) If a pupils parent / carer derelicts in his/ her duties to ensure the completion of compulsory schooling he/ she shall be sentenced to fine for dereliction of a duty in ensuring of completion of compulsory schooling.

Section 47: Supportive Activities

(i) Library club and other activities closely relating to education may be arranged in conjunction with basic education.

Section 47A: Pupil Association

(i) A school assigned by the local authority may have a student association composed of the pupils to promote joint action, influence and participation of the pupils in matter relating to pupils.

Section 48: Before and after school activities

(School relation and dynamics with the neighbourhood society analysis)

(i) The purpose of before and after school activities is to support the schools and the homes educational work and the development of the Child's emotional life and ethical growth.

In addition, before and after school activity in society prevent exclusion and promote inclusion.

II. South Africa Basic Education Law, Amendment Act, No. 15, 2011

(i) Compulsory attendance 7 years to 15 years or nine grades.

(ii) Minister determine age of compulsory attendance for learners with SEN (Special Education Need).

(iii) Every member of the executive council must ensure that there are enough school places so that every child who lives in her province can attend school.

(iv) If a learner who is subject to compulsory attendance is not enrolled at or fails to attend a school, the head of Department may-

   (a) Investigate the circumstances of the learner's absence from school.

   (b) Take appropriate measures to remedy the situation; and

   (c) Failing such a remedy, issue a written notice to the parent of the learner.

(v) Subject to this Act and any other applicable law-

(a) Any parent who, without just cause and after a written notice from the head of department, fails to admit his ward is guilty of an offence and liable on conviction to a fine or to imprisonment for a period not exceeding six months.

(vi) Exemption from compulsory attendance - Head of Department may exempt a learner entirely, partially or conditionally from compulsory school attendance, if it is in the best interest of the learner.

(vii) A public school must admit learners and serve their educational requirement without unfairly discriminating in any way.

(viii) No test for admission.

(ix) In determining the placement of a learner with special education needs, the Head of Department and principal must take in to account the right and wishes of the parent of such learner.

(x) No form of vital discrimination may be practiced in implementing language policy.

(xi) A recognised sign language has the status of an official language at a public school.

(xii) Unless authorised by the principal for legitimate educational purposes, no person may bring dangerous object or illegal drug on to school premises or have such object or drug in his or her possession on school premises or during any school activity.

(xiii) The governing body may, on reasonable grounds and as precautionary measure suspend a Learner who is suspected in a serious misconduct from attending school but may only enforce such suspension after the learner has been granted a reasonable opportunity to make representation to it in relation to such suspension.

(xiv) No person may administer corporal punishment at a school to a learner.

(xv) A person who contravenes this suspension is guilty of an offence and liable on conviction to a sentence which could be enforced for assault.

(xvi) A representative council of learners at the school must be established at every public school. Enrolling in the eighth grade or higher, and such council is the only recognised and legitimate representative learner body at the school.

(xvii) A public school may be an ordinary public school; a public school for learners with special education needs or a public school that provides education with a specialised course on talent, including sports, performing arts or creative arts.

(xviii) If the HOD determines on reasonable ground that a governing body has ceased to perform function allocated to it in term of this act or has failed to perform one or more of such function, he/ she must appoint sufficient persons to perform all such function or one or more of such functions as the case may be, for a period not exceeding three months.

(xix) Funding of public school: The state must fund public school from public head on an equitable basis in order to ensure the proper exercise of the right of learners to education and the redress of past inequality in education provision.

(xx) School fees at public schools-

(a) Subject to this act, school fees may be determined and charged at a public school only if a resolution to do so has been adopted by a majority of parents attending the meeting;

(b) A resolution convened in the above provision must provide for;

(c) The amount of school fees to be charged;

(d) Equitable criteria and procedures for the total, partial or conditional exemption of parents who are unable to pay school fees; and

(e) A school budget that reflects the established trends of non-payment of school fees, and the total partial or conditional exemptions granted to parents in terms of the regulations.

(xxi) Parents liability for payment of school fees

(a) A parent liable to pay the school fees determined as in earlier clause unless or to the extent that he or she has been exempted from payment in term of this act.

(b) A parent may appeal to head of department against the decision of a governing body regarding the exemption of such parent from such fees.

(xxii) Registration of learner for education at home-

(a) A parent may apply to the head of department for the registration of a learner to receive education at the learner's home.

(b) The Head of Department must register a learner as contemplated in above provision if he or she is satisfied that -

(c) The registration is in the interests of the learner;

(d) The education likely to be received by the learner at home- (i) will meet the minimum requirements of the curriculum at public schools; and (ii) will be of a standard not inferior to the standard of education provided at public schools; and

(e) The parent will comply with any other reasonable conditions set by the Head of Department.

III. Main features of RTE in China

Chapter 1- General Provisions

(1) Nine-year compulsory education for school age children and adolescents.

(2) Compulsory education means education which is uniformly provided by the state and which all the school age children and adolescents must receive and constitutes a public welfare undertaking, which must be guaranteed by state. No tuition miscellaneous fees shall be charged for compulsory education ensures implementation of the system of compulsory education.

(3) State council and the local people's government at above the county level shall rationally allocate educational resources, promote balanced development of compulsory education, help the schools started on weak foundation to improve the conditions for school running, and adopt measures to ensure that compulsory education is provided in rural areas and areas inhabited by ethnic groups and that the school age children and adolescents who are from families with financial

difficulties or who are disabled to relieve compulsory education.

(4) All government organisations and individuals shall have the right to inform the state organs concerned violation of this law or lodge complaint against such violations with the said organs.

(5) Where a major event in violation of this law occurs, which impedes provision of CE thus exerting a great impact on the society, the leading persons of the peoples government concerned or the administrative department for education of the peoples government shall admit his mistake and resign.

Chapter 2- Students

(6) Compulsory education at the age of six. For children in areas where conditions do not exist for children to do so, the beginning of their schooling may be postponed to the age of seven.

(7) School age children and adolescents shall be exempted from the entrance examination. The local people's government at various level shall ensure that school age children and adolescent enroll in school near the places where there residence is registered.

(8) The residence committees and Villiers committees' shall assist the government in successfully urging school age children and adolescent to enroll in school.

(9) No employing units shall employ a school children or adolescent who are expected to receive compulsory education.

Chapter 3- Schools

(10) Local peoples government at or above the county level shall on the basic of such factor as the number of school age children and adolescent and the places of their residence and its administrative area and according to relevant state regulations, formulate and adjust the plan for the establishment of school.

(11) People government at or above the country level may in light of need boarding school to ensure that the school age children and adolescent to who live for from school receive compulsory education.

(12) Central government shall in light of need, establish schools in economically underdeveloped areas to enroll school age children and adolescent of ethnic groups.

(13) Peoples government at or above the county level and the administrative department for education shall promote balanced development among schools by narrowing the difference in the conditions for school running and shall not divide the schools in to key and non-key schools. And the schools shall not divide the classes in to key and non-key classes.

Chapter 4- Teacher

(14) Teacher shall be respected by entire society.

(15) Teacher shall treat students equally in instruction and teaching, and pay attention of the individual difference of students to promote their full development.

(16) Teachers engaged in special education shall enjoy subsidies for special posts. Teachers working in areas inhabited by ethnic groups or in outlying or poverty stricken areas shall enjoy subsidies for working under tough conditions or in poverty-stricken areas.

Chapter 5- Instruction and Teaching

(17) Instruction and teaching shall be carried out in conformity with the pattern of education and the characteristics of students to the need of all student, be oriented to the need of all students and designed to impart knowledge to them by organically integrating moral, intellectual, physical and aesthetic education in instruction and teaching, with special attention paid to developing their of independent thinking, creativity and practice in order to enable them to develop in all round way.

Chapter 6 - Guarantee of funds

(18) The state places compulsory education completely within the scope of financial guarantee and the funds for compulsory education shall be guaranteed by the state council and the local people's governments at various levels according to the provisions of this law.

The percentage of increase in government funds allotted for compulsory education by the state council and the local peoples governments of various levels shall be higher than the percentage of increase in regular government revenues in order to ensure the gradual increase in the average amount of funds for compulsory education per student in school, in the salaries of the teaching staff and in the average amount of funds per student for public use.

(19) The state encourages public organisations and individuals to make donations to compulsory education and encourages the establishment of foundations for compulsory education in accordance with the state regulations governing the administration of foundations.

Chapter 7- Legal Responsibility

(20) Under one of the following circumstances, a school shall be ordered to make rectification within a time limit by the administrative department for education of the peoples government at the country level, and if the circumstances are serious, the person directly responsible shall be punished according to law:

(i) Refusing to admit to the classes corresponding to the levels of the disabled school age children and adolescents who are capable of receiving regular education;

(ii) Dividing classes in to key and non-key ones;

(iii) Expelling students in violation of the provisions in this law; or

(iv) Using textbooks which have not been examined and for which no approval has been obtained.

(21) The parents or other statutory guardians of school age children or adolescents who without justifiable reasons, fail to send them to schools to receive compulsory education according to the local peoples government at the town or township of the administrative department for education of the peoples government or department to make ratification within a time limit.

(22) Under one of the following circumstances, an organisation or individual shall be punished according to the provisions of relevant laws and administrative regulations.

(i) Coercing or cajoling school age children or adolescents who should receive compulsory education into forfeiting schooling or dropping out of school.

(ii) Illegally employing school age children or adolescents who should receive compulsory education.

(iii) Publishing textbooks which have not been examined and for which to approval has been obtained according to law.

IV. RTE in Sri Lanka

(1) Compulsory education in Sri Lanka enacted in 1997.

(2) Enrollment and attendance of children between 5 and 14 years with attendance committee at school level to monitor attendance.

(3) Equity in education- free education is given in all government and government -assisted schools and also up to the first degree level in university, free text books, free school uniform, subsidized transport are provided and children in grade one classes where malnutrition has been prevalent are provided with a nutritious meal. The deserving students from low income families are also provided with bursaries to meet their other expenses, which continue up to university level. These are in addition to a widespread social safety including free health services poor relief and many other subsidies.

(4) Mismatch between education and employment:

Attempts were made to stream children at the end of primary and basic education stage to academic, technical and vocational streams. However, these proposals were not acceptable to a public who had seen in the past that academic success had led to social mobility. Now efforts are being made to provide a practical element to general education through the development of competencies.

(5) An inquiring mind ability for analysis and reasoning the application of knowledge to practical problems and a problem solving approach, knowledge and interest in contemporary social and economic developments in the country. Capacity for leadership and team work, a work ethos with values of productivity and discipline imparted through appropriate learning experiences in suitable technical, vocational subject and most important good communication

skills, both oral as well as written, even in the mother tongue, not to mention English.

(6) Learning Process-

Such a transformation can be brought about by changing the methodology of teaching and learning rather than through the content of education. Of course that does not discount the importance of science and technology in the modern contest. But use of activity based learning techniques such as project work, assignments, discovery methods etc. Will sharpen the general skills of students.

(7) Measures taken

(i) Policy of providing a primary school within 2 km from the residence of any child and providing a school having classes up to G. C. E. (O/L) within 4 km from the residence of any child has been implemented with only a few exceptions.

(ii) Provision of free text books from grade 1 to G. C. E (O/L), free school uniform to all school children, subsidized transport to children and mid day meals to children in schools in selected locations.

(iii) Provision of 10,000 bursaries every year to talented children from low income families to support their transition to secondary education.

(iv) Enforcement of compulsory education regulations for children 5-14 with effect from January 1998.

(a) School attendance committees.

(b) School attendance monitoring committees.

(v) Establishment of literacy centers under non-formal setting.

(vi) Capacity building of NIE with UNICEF assistance to examine the curriculum and text books from a gender perspective and providing support to develop more gender sensitised educational material.

(vii) Safe drinking water and separate toilets for girls and boys are encouraged in schools.

(viii) Girls and boys are encouraged to participate in extracurricular activities on an equal footing.

(ix) Teachers are sensitised on gender issues during the pre-service and in-service training.

(8) Flexible learning opportunities and life skills development-

The junior secondary state curriculum has introduced life competencies as a subject and practical work and work on small project as an important element. Activity rooms were proposed to be established in schools to enable students to learn by doing things by themselves, using simple tools and learning simple techniques. In the curriculum for secondary senior stage of GCE O/L. Technical subject to help student continue learning of life skills, practical work has been made compulsory in the GCE A/L curriculum. It was proposed by the 1998 reform that links be developed between the school system and the vocational and technical training system to provide flexible learning opportunities to student. Career guidance and counseling has been introduced at this stage in order to provide advice to students to enable them to select avenues most suited to their capabilities. Community learning centers have been established under non-formal sector to provide flexible learning opportunities and life skills development to children not being able to attend school.

The recent proposal by the national education commission includes changes in the secondary education curriculum in order to improve the life competencies of students.

The current practical technical skills subject area in grades 6 to 9 will be restructured and renamed as technical skills which cover the areas namely, Graphic Arts, Computer Literacy (IT), elementary technology, agriculture, and food preparation.

(9) Acquiring a common basic of human values

The schools are expected to play an active role in promoting moral, ethical and spiritual values. Value Education encompasses the moral and spiritual values, ideas and concepts derived from the religion followed by an individual that has a bearing on the commitment to personal and social behaviour.

The totality of experience provided by the curriculum implemented in schools should promote the inculcation of values in students. This should not be viewed as a separate subject.

(10) Subjects in Elementary Education

(a) Introduction of history, civics and geography as separate subjects in grades 6 to 9 to replace environmental studies in grade 6 and social studies in grades 7 to 11.

(b) Integration of generic skills such as critical thinking, initiative, problem solving, team work and human values in the content, activities and teaching learning experiences.

(c) Introduction of a new subject called technology with 6 options and practical components in grades 12 and 13 (GCE-AL).

(11) Teacher Training

Pre-service teacher education thus becoming an essential requirement in recruiting non-graduate teachers to the system made redundant the 16 teacher's colleges and the large-scale distance teacher education programme of the national institute of education (NIE) that provided initial teacher education to practicing teachers, recognising the importance of continuing teachers education to practicing teachers. Recognising the importance of continuing teacher education the same reforms also paved the way for the establishment of 100 teacher centers so that each educational zone of the country had at least one teacher centre. The purpose of this new initiative was to provide short term non-residential continuing teacher education to upgrade teacher skills at least once in every seven years. Identifying the need for residential continuing teacher education of a longer duration, a decision was also made to retain some of the teachers college as teacher education institutes. Importance of physical facilities of the restricted in- service teacher education institutes are also now provided adequate facilities and suitable atmosphere for both initial and continuing teacher education.

Notes

1. http://shodhganga.inflibnet.ac.in/bitstream/10603/8116/12/12_chapter%203.pdf
2. Joshi, S.K., (2013), 'Journey of Right to Education: A Historical Perceptive' article in an International peer reviewed scholarly research journal for interdisciplinary studies, Vol. II/IX, p. 757.
3. Juneja, Nalini (2003), 'Constitutional Amendments to make Education a fundamental Right Issues for a follow-up Legislation', New Delhi: NUEPA, pp. 15-17.

4. Joshi, S. K. (2013), 'Journey of Right to Education: A Historical Perceptive' article in an International peer reviewed scholarly research journal for interdisciplinary studies, Vol. II/IX, p. 757.

5. I. Narendra Kumar and S. Siva Prasad (2012), 'Right to Education and equal Opportunity in India' In: Rao Pulla, (ed.) *Right to Education as An Inclusive Policy*, New Delhi: ABD Publishers, p. 29.

6. Joshi, S.K. (2013), 'Journey of Right to Education: A Historical Perceptive' article in an International peer reviewed scholarly research journal for interdisciplinary studies, Vol. II/IX, p. 759.

7. Joshi, S.K. (2013), 'Journey of Right to Education: A Historical Perceptive' article in an International peer reviewed scholarly research journal for interdisciplinary studies, Vol. II/IX, p. 759.

8. I. Narendra Kumar and S. Siva Prasad (2012), 'Right to Education and equal Opportunity in India' In: Rao Pulla, (ed.) *Right to Education as An Inclusive Policy*, New Delhi: ABD Publishers, p. 29.

9. http://shodhganga.inflibnet.ac.in/bitstream/10603/8116/12/12_chapter%203.pdf

10. http://www.ashanet.org/campaigns/rte/HistoryOfRightToEducation.html

Chapter - 3

Research Methodology

3.1 Conceptual Framework and Need of the Study

Conceptually the RTE is a revolutionary act fulfilling the ultimate aim of constitutionalism. The inclusiveness of SC and ST students in education and its implications for RTE proposes to find the fulfillment of constitutional provisions, especially the strengths and also the lacunae that shall be apparent during implementation.

Inclusiveness is the catchword of the eleventh five - year plan signifying the nation's urge to include the socio-economic upliftment of the SC, ST and OBC to the pedestal of the main agenda of planning and growth. Inclusiveness is a process of addressing and responding to the needs of the socio-economically underprivileged sections of the society in order to bring them at par. Inclusive education is a process of addressing and responding to the socio-economically and psychologically tugged learning abilities and educational opportunities of the underprivileged sections of our society. Inclusive education incorporates the principle of access which should go to become access to quality education. And at the core of inclusive education is the right to education. This is expressed in the ground-level fact of enrollment and quality of education, which in turn has to do a lot of catching-up. The SC students accounted for 10.7% in 1980-81 which rose to 19.55% in 2014-15. Regarding enrollment of ST students it rose from 3.58% in 1980-81 to 9.76% in 2014-15.[1]

The study focuses on the educational participation of the SC and ST students under the Right to Education taking into consideration their socio-cultural and economic constraints and the possible policy lacunae regarding SC and ST in the RTE and also the implementation issues that could warrant amendments as experience is gained. Inclusiveness shall become operational by an empirical exposure of the implementation of the RTE.

3.2 Statement of the Problem

Statement of the problem is 'Inclusiveness of SC and ST students: Implications for Right to Education'. The problem involves primary education of the SC and ST students under the Right to Education it also involves implications vis-à-vis strengths and policy suggestions over possible lacunae in the right to education.

3.3 Aim of the Project

The aim of the project is to gauge the level of social and educational inclusiveness of SC and ST students in the process of primary education manifested through the provisions of the Right to Free and Compulsory Education Act, direct and indirect. It also includes finding the strengths and lacunae regarding inclusiveness of SC and ST students along with suggesting suitable policy orientation.

3.4 Research Questions

(1) What is the evolution of the RTE and what are the direct and indirect SC and ST students related provisions in the RTE?

(2) What are the implement ability and possible socio-economic constraints of SC and ST students regarding major RTE provisions?

(3) What are the difficulties faced by teachers in and what are their views on, implementation of various RTE provisions, especially regarding the educational inclusiveness of SC and ST students?

(4) Can the RTE financing model be reviewed with best interests of the SC and ST students?

(5) What are the strengths and lacunae in the various provisions of RTE regarding SC and ST students' educational inclusion?

3.5 Coverage

(i) Universe of the study

All schools of Pune and Beed districts of Maharashtra is the universe of this study. Researcher selected the schools by purposive sample method.While selecting the schools the researcher tried to accommodate all type of schools for the fieldwork. Criteria and reasoning of the selection of schools is as follows:

(ii) Schools selected from both districts

The Right to Education Act 2009 came in to force on 1st April 2010 in India. Every child between the age of 6 to 14 years has the right to free and compulsory education in a neighbourhood school till the completion of elementary education. The act is applicable to all schools established, owned, or controlled by the appropriate government local authority as well as all aided and unaided schools except unaided private minority schools.

In Maharashtra, this act came in to force from 2011. Socio-educational and economic conditions of the regions may affect the implementation status of the right to education.Therefore, for the comparative understanding of the implementation of this act the researcher selected two distinct districts from Maharashtra - (1) Pune and (2) Beed. The first is an educationally developed district while the second is not.

All schools (which come under RTE) of the Pune and Beed districts come under the universe of this study. Researcher visited 33 schools and these schools were selected by the purposive sample method. In all selected schools18(54.55%) were from Pune and 15(45.45%) schools were from Beed district. It was an attempt to give almost fifty percent representations to each district in this study.

(iii) Area-wise selection of schools

For better understanding of the implementation of the RTE act the researcher visited schools from rural, urban, semi-urban and tribal areas. It is perceived that issues regarding the implementation of this act are different as per regions. Therefore, the researcher selected the schools from different regions.

Area-wise selection of schools

Sr. No.	Area	Pune	Beed	Total	Percent
1.	Rural	05	07	12	36.36
2.	Semi Urban	00	02	02	6.06
3.	Urban	11	06	17	51.52
4.	Tribal Area	02	00	02	6.06
Total		**18**	**15**	**33**	**100.00**

Area-wise percentage of the selected schools is as follows- schools from rural areas were 36.36%, schools from semi-urban area were 6.06%, from urban areas 51.52% schools were covered and 2(6.06%) schools were covered from tribal areas.

(iv) Class level-wise school selection

Students of 8th and 9th standards are the target group of this study but in the case of unavailability of these students, the students from lower standards were considered as a unit of the study. Therefore, researcher selected the schools with primary, primary with upper primary, secondary and upper primary with secondary levels. The class level-wise numbers of schools are as follows:

Class Level-wise number of Schools

Sr. No.	Level of school	Pune	Beed	Total	Percent
1.	Primary	03	00	03	9.09
2.	Upper Primary	02	00	02	6.06
3.	Secondary	11	08	19	57.58
4.	Primary, Upper Primary & Secondary	00	02	02	6.06
5.	Primary & Secondary	02	00	02	6.06
6.	Upper Primary & Secondary	00	05	05	15.15
Total		**18**	**15**	**33**	**100.00**

In all schools 57.58% schools were up to secondary level, 15.15% schools were upper primary and secondary level, only 9% schools were primary level. Upper primary level 6.06%, upper primary and secondary level 6.06%, primary, upper primary and secondary level schools were 6.06%.

(v) Management wise schools

For the better understanding of RTE act, the researcher tried to cover all types of schools. Issues regarding the implementation of this act seem to there in all schools but particularly in privet schools. Therefore, for the comparative evaluation of the implementation of the RTE act in various types of schools the researcher selected all types of schools. Management wise numbers of schools are as follows-

Management-wise classification of schools

Sr. No.	School Management	Pune	Beed	Total	Percent
1.	Tribal Department	03	00	03	9.09
2.	Z.P.	00	04	04	12.12
3.	Municipal Corporation	02	00	02	6.06
4.	Nagar Palika	01	00	01	3.03
5.	Private-Aided	05	08	13	39.39
6.	Private-Un Aided	06	03	09	27.27
7.	Poona cantonment board	01	00	01	3.03
Total		**18**	**15**	**33**	**100.00**

Table and figure shows the management-wise proportion of schools covered in this study. The private aided schools were 36.36 percent, private unaided schools were 27.27%, and schools of Zilha Parishad were 12.12%. Schools of municipal corporation, Nagar Palika, Tribal Department and Poona Cantonment Board were also covered.

(vi) Medium of instruction

It is perceived that mostly private un-aided and English medium schools have implementation issues regarding admission under RTE act. For the medium-wise comparative understanding the researcher covered various medium-wise schools as follows:

Medium of instruction

Sr. No.	Medium	Pune	Beed	Total	Percent
1.	Marathi	07	08	15	45.45
2.	English	05	01	06	18.18
3.	Semi- English	04	04	08	24.24
4.	Urdu	02	02	04	12.12
Total		**18**	**15**	**33**	**100.00**

The above figure and table show the medium-wise schools covered in this study. In the schools surveyed Marathi medium schools were 45.45%, English medium schools were 18.18%, schools of semi-English were 24.24 and Urdu medium schools were 12.12 percent.

(vii) Unit-size of the study

Persons who are directly or indirectly involved with the Right to Education Act are the units for this study. Headmaster, teacher, students, member of school management committee and the parents are directly engaged with the RTE act. Responses from all of these are very important to know the actual status and issues of the implementation of this act. Following table shows the number of persons interviewed in this study.

Unit size of the study

Sample	Pune		Total	Beed		Total	All
	Male	Female		Male	Female		
Headmasters	07	11	18	14	01	15	33
Teachers	07	15	22	13	02	15	37
Students	41	66	107	44	46	90	197
SMC Members	05	09	14	10	04	14	28
9th std students	06	13	19	06	07	13	32
Age-appropriate admitted students	02	04	06	04	01	05	11
Parents	07	08	15	02	11	13	28
Total							**366**

There were 366 respondents interviewed in this research. In that the Headmasters were 33 in number, percentage of the headmaster respondents from Pune is 54.55% and from Beed district 45.45%. Proportion of female Headmaster respondents in Pune is more than the male. Whereas, the situation in Beed totally contrast to Pune.

The researcher interacted with two experienced teachers from each selected school. Teacher respondents are 37 from both districts, in which 22(59.46%) were from Pune and 15(40.54%) from Beed district. In Beed the teacher male-female ratio is in favour of the female teachers. The researcher interacted with 28 members of school management committee which included 14 (50%) from Pune and 14(50%) from Beed district.

The researcher collected the information from 197 students of 8th standard. The researcher selected seven students from each school making up 107 students from Pune and 97 students from Beed District.

Thirty two students have been interviewed from the 9th standard. In this 19 students were from Pune and 13 from Beed district.

In the age appropriate admitted students six were from Pune and five from Beed.

In the parent respondents 15 were from Pune and 13 from Beed district.

(viii) Social Category of the respondents

This study was taken up to find out the status of implementation of various provisions of the RTE act for the disadvantaged children, and specifically the SC and ST students. Therefore, students from SC and ST category are the target group of this study. However, for the comparative perusal of this act the researcher purposely selected respondents from various social categories as follows:

Social category of the respondents

Units of the study	SC	ST	OBC	NT	Minority (Muslim, Jain & Christian)	SBC	Open	Total
Headmasters	07 (21.21%)	--	03 (9.09%)	03 (9.09%)	09 (27.27%)	--	11 (33.33%)	33
Teachers	02 (5.41%)	01 (2.70%)	06 (16.22%)	06 (16.22%)	10 (27.03%)	--	12 (32.43%)	37
SMC Members	03 (10.71%)	02 (7.14%)	07 (25%)	03 (10.71%)	04 (14.29%)	--	09 (32.14%)	23
Parents	05 (17.86%)	--	06 (21.43%)	02 (7.14%)	10 (35.71%)	--	05 (17.86%)	28
Students	63 (31.98%)	23 (11.68%)	23 (11.68%)	26 (13.20%)	39 (19.80%)	2 (1.02%)	21 (10.66%)	197
9th std students	14 (43.75%)	05 (15.63%)	02 (6.25%)	03 (9.38%)	05 (15.63%)	--	03 (9.38%)	32
Age- appropriate admitted students	01 (9.09%)	01 (9.09%)	01 (9.09%)	02 (18.18%)	05 (45.45%)	--	01 (9.09%)	11

Above table shows the social category wise-proportion of the respondents. In the 33 headmaster respondents 21.21% were from SC, 9.09% were OBC and DNT category, 27.27% were from Muslim, Jain, Sikh and Christian minority and 33.33% were from open category.

Of the teacher respondents32.43% were from open category, 18.92% from OBC, 16.22% were from DNT category, 5.41% from SC, 2.70% were ST and 27.03% from Muslim, Jain, Sikh and Christian minority.

Of the school management committee respondents 32.14% were from open category, 10.71% from SC and NT, 7.14% from ST and 14.29% from Muslim, Jain, Sikh and Christian minority.

Of the 28 parents 17.86% were from open category, 21.43% from OBC, 17.86% were SC, 35.71% from Muslim, Jain, Sikh and Christian minority and 7.14% were DNT.

Besides headmaster, teacher, SMC member and parents the researcher interacted with seven students in each school who belonged to different social categories.It was an attempt to know the opinion of students from different socio-economic background regarding implementation and implications of the RTE act. Therefore, the researcher purposively selected students from different categories. The student respondents respectively, 31.98% were from SC category, 17.77% were from open category, 11.68% from OBC and DNT category. While 11.68% were from ST, 19.80% from Muslim, Jain, Sikh and Christian minority and two students from SBC category. The researcher also interacted with students from 9th standard and the age-appropriate admitted students.

3.6 Collection of Data

Researcher collected the data from both - primary and secondary sources.

(i) Primary Data

Researcher used the interview schedule for the collection of the primary data. Interview schedule is a reliable source of the data collection. The investigator can observe and probe the reality while filling the schedules. The researcher used interview schedule as a tool to collect the primary data in order to avoid situations where the respondents viz. parents, students, SMC members could not write the questionnaires themselves.

(ii) Secondary Data

There searcher also used the secondary data to prepare the report.

There are a lot of studies and literature on the Right to Education which was usedas secondary source material. In the secondary sources the researcher used reference books, research papers, working papers, published/unpublished documents regarding right to education, legal arguments on RTE, unpublished M. Phil and Ph.D. thesis and e-material etc.

3.7 Tools and Techniques

The researcher collected information from headmasters, teachers, students, members of the school management committee and parents. Interview schedule was the tool for the collection of data. The researcher purposely used this tool to observe ground level reality. While collecting the data through interview schedules the investigator asked the questions and noted the given answers leading to a collection of a reliable data from the respondents.

3.8 Analysis of Data

The data was collected through qualitative and quantitative methods. Coding of the data was done to facilitate data entry. All the data was analyzed and tables prepared.

Notes

1. School Education in India, Flash Statistics 2015, National University of Educational Planning and Administration, New Delhi.

Chapter - 4

Elementary Education of Scheduled Castes and Scheduled Tribes in India

Education plays an important role in the development of a nation in general and the individual in particular. Quality primary education is regarded as the foundation of nation building. Education is the powerful tool for the upliftment of the socio-economically backward and marginalised sections of the society. It promotes individual freedom and empowerment and yields important development benefits. Many social reformers especially, Mahatma Phule, Dr Babasaheb Ambedkar underlined the importance of education. Dr Ambedkar said that 'The backward classes have come to realise that after all education is the greatest material benefit for which they can fight. We may forego material benefits of civilisation, but we cannot forego our right and opportunities to reap the benefit of the highest education to the fullest extent. That the importance of this question from the point of view of the backward classes, who have just realised that without education their existence is not safe.'[1]

However, it is a fact that millions of children especially from backward classes are remaining without education due to various socio-economic conditions. 'Of the nearly 200 million children in the age group between 6 to 14 years, more than half do not complete eight years of elementary education; they either enroll or they drop out of school. Of those who do complete eight years of schooling, the achievement levels of a large percentage, in languages and mathematics, is unacceptably low. It is no wonder that a majority of the excluded and non-achievers come from the most deprived sections of the society – dalits, other backward classes, tribals, women, muslims and financially backward – precisely those who are supposed to be empowered through education.'[2] The Right to Education Act, 2009 guarantees free and compulsory education to every child in the 6-14 age group. However, due to a number of implementation issues and also challengeable basic provisions of the RTE the practical benefits to the disadvantaged and weaker sections, SC and ST students, is a matter of research.

In this chapter the researcher tries to put focus on actual status of elementary education of backward classes, especially on the elementary education of SC and ST students.

4.1 Development of Elementary Education post-Independence

In independent India, central and state governments jointly carried the responsibility of education. The various articles of the Indian Constitution were directive for provision of education. Through the National Policy on Education (NPE) 1968 and subsequently by NPE 1986, attempts were being made to adopt a common structure of schooling across the country. The general pattern adopted at the national level, commonly known as the 10+2+3 pattern, envisages a broad-based general education for all pupils during the first ten years of schooling. Diversification of courses takes place only at the higher secondary level and is reliant on students successfully completing the secondary school examination. Of these ten years of schooling, the first eight years are termed 'elementary education', and this should broadly correspond to the compulsory education period of 6-14 years of age.[3]

Elementary education forms the foundation for all levels of learning and development. It empowers and equips individuals with analytical capabilities, instills confidence and fortifies them with determination to achieve goal-setting competencies. It, therefore, plays pivotal role in improving the socio-economic condition of the nation. For any country to grow, it is imperative that it has in place a strong elementary school driven education system.

Universalisation of elementary education is our constitutional obligation. However, this was targeted to have been achieved within a period of 10 years from the date of the adoption of our constitution. But a majority of states in India are still struggling and are still far away from this goal. India has made huge progress in terms of increasing primary education quantitatively, but inclusion-wise we are far away.

Here we consider the growth of educational institutions from 1950-51 to 2013-14. Since independence, India has made impressive progress in terms of growth of educational institutions at different levels. During 1950-51 to 2013-14 primary and upper primary schools increased more than 5.25 times. The recognised educational institutes increased by more than 6.25 times.

4.2 Institutions by Management

It is government responsibility to make available education for all citizen of India. Our constitution provides for education in the Article 45 of part IV.The constitution declared that the state shall endeavour to provide, within a period of ten years from the commencement of this constitution, for free and compulsory education to children below the age of 14. It means the provision of elementary education to all children was the responsibility of the government. However, the government is slowly moving away from this responsibility, which is evident by the higher increase in number of privately managed schools as compared to public schools.

The data indicates the percentage of government and private schools in 2009-10 and 2013-14. The number of government schools decreased by 1.81 percent in Maharashtra and 4.86 percent at the national level. On the other hand, private unaided schools increased by 3.36 percent in this period. 'Besides that, enrolment in the government schools also decreased by 7.76 percent in 2014-15 as compared to figures of 2007-08, but it increased by 34.84 percent in the private schools in the same period'[4]. The demand for schooling has increased among the people of all the strata of society, including the marginalised, over the years, but standards of government schools are declining considerably. Despite an increase in enrolment, the content and process of schooling and teaching practices are not only degrading but also bypassing the SC and ST students. Besides, to improve the quality and quantity in education the government is not putting in the best efforts and as an effect encouraging privatisation of education. It is a serious obstacle for our constitutional objective of universalisation of education.

4.3 Enrolment in Elementary Education

Enrolment in the school at various levels indicates the educational progress of the state. We can predict the direction of the educational progress of the state by comparing the enrollment of the particular age group and population projection of that specific group.

The data shows the enrolment of SC, ST and all categories in elementary education. Between 2000-01 to 2013-14 the enrolment of all categories and SC and ST is constantly increasing. The enrolment of the all categories reached at the highest level in the 2011-12 (199.1 million) and then declined to 198.9 million in 2013-14. The overall increase in enrolment in elementary education during the period 2000-01 to 2013-14 was 42.3 million.

The enrolment of the SC and ST categories is also increasing constantly from 2000-01 to 2011-12. In the year of 2011-12, the enrollment of the SC category reached at the highest level (39.4 million) and the ST category (21.7 million) then declined to 39.2 million in 2013-14 of SC and 21.7 million of ST category respectively. During the year 2013-14, the number of SC children enrolled as percentage of total enrolment in elementary education was 16.6 percent while the share of SC population in the total population was 19.72 percent in 2011 (Census, 2011). It means still 3.12 percent of SC children remain without education. Between 2000-01 and 2013-14, the enrolment of ST children in elementary education increased by 7 million (from 14.1 million to 21.1 million).

The percentage of SC, ST enrolment is lower as compared to total enrolment. Following data indicates the percentage of these categories in total enrolment.

Percentage of SC and ST Enrolment to Total Enrolment

Level/Year	2009-10		2010-11		2011-12		2012-13		2013-14		2014-15		2015-16	
	SC	ST	SC	ST	SC	ST	SC	ST	SC	ST	SC	ST	SC	ST
Primary Level	26.01	14.92	26.93	14.85	28.69	15.31	27.03	15.02	19.88	11.09	19.93	10.83	19.94	10.64
Upper Primary Level	10.87	5.16	11.30	5.42	12.24	5.61	12.06	6.04	19.41	9.73	19.55	9.76	19.49	9.81
Secondary Level	5.44	2.07	5.70	2.17	6.61	2.53	NA	NA	18.42	8.58	18.67	8.49	18.68	8.49
Higher Secondary Level	2.77	1.02	3.00	1.09	3.80	1.29	NA	NA	17.38	6.25	17.59	6.45	17.33	6.77

Source – School Education in India 2009-10 to 2015-16 - UDISE NA- Not Available.

The percentage of the children from SC and ST community in total enrolment. The percentage of SC children in total enrolment is better than ST community. Moreover, the percentage of ST children has been decreasing with the increased level of education. The percentage of SC children in total enrolment is also lower and has been decreasing with the increasing level of education. The percentage of SC and ST children in the primary level enrolment is decreasing with every subsequent year, with the exceptions of 2011 to 2013, but increasing with the increased level of education and year.

4.4 Gross Enrolment Ratio in Elementary Education

Gross Enrolment Ratio (GER) is defined as the percentage of the enrolment in elementary education (Classes I-VIII and age 6 to below 14 years). The Gross Enrolment Ratios for the Elementary education (I-VIII) stage in respect of all categories of students and students of the SC and ST category are presented below.Enrolment in elementary education includes under-age and overage children. Hence, the percentage may be more than 100% in some cases.

Gross Enrolment ratio in Elementary Education

Year	Gross Enrolment Ratio		
	All Category	SC	ST
2000-01	81.6	86.8	88
2001-02	82.4	85.6	88.9
2003-04	84.8	83.4	86.1
2005-06	94.9	102	106.7
2007-08	100.3	108.4	112.7
2009-10	102.5	113.5	118.9
2011-12	94.7	110.8	114.5
2013-14	97	107.7	105.5

Based on the available data the Gross enrolment ratio in elementary education for all categories (Classes I-VIII; Age 6 to below 14 years) has increased by 15.4 percentage points during the period 2001-02 to 2013-14. While the Gross Enrolment Ratio (GER) for SC children in elementary education has increased by 20.9 percentage points (from 86.8 percent to 107.7 percent) between 2000-01 and 2013-14. The Gross Enrolment Ratio (GER) in elementary education for ST children increased by 17.5 percentage points (from 88 percent to 105.5 percent) during the period 2000-01 to 2013-14.

It appears from above data that, the GER of SC and ST slightly better than all categories from the year of 2000-01 to 2013-14.

4.5 Drop Out Rates in Elementary Education

The drop out rate represents percentage of pupils who drop out from a given grade or cycle or level of education in a given school year. 'The issue of dropouts or out of school-children is going to be a major concern. According to a calculation of National University of Education Planning and Administration (NUEPA), in 2008-09, total enrolment for primary level (I-V class) was 134.4 million but it dropped by 53.4 million when it reached to upper primary level.'[5] It means dropout from education is the major issue in the current circumstances. There could be several social, economic and cultural issues behind this drop out phenomenon which is faced particularly by girls and children from the SC and ST category. These issues must be solved for universalisation of education. The category-wise and education level-wise dropout rates are presented as follows:

Drop Out Rates in School Education

Level/ Year	Classes I-V			Classes I-VIII			Classes I-X		
	SC	ST	All Categories	SC	ST	All Categories	SC	ST	All Categories
1990-91	49.4	62.5	42.6	67.8	78.6	60.9	85.0	85.0	71.3
2001-02	45.2	52.3	NA	60.7	68.7	NA	72.7	81.2	NA
2010-11	27.1	35.6	27.4	43.4	55.0	40.8	56.1	70.9	49.2
2011-12	23.5	35.3	22.3	40.2	57.2	40.8	55.3	65.9	50.3
2012-13(P)	19.2	32.3	21.3	39.7	49.2	39.0	52.5	62.7	50.4
2013-14(P)	16.6	31.3	19.8	38.8	48.2	36.3	50.1	62.4	47.4

P : Provisional, NA : Not Available
Source - Educational Statistics at a Glance, MHRD: New Delhi, 2014.

The drop out rates of all categories at all levels indicated in the above table shows a decreases on large scale as compared to the figures of 1990-91 to 2013-14. While the drop out rates of SC and ST at all levels are slightly high as compared to all categories and has constantly increased as per educational level. The drop out rates of the SC and ST on the secondary level are too high as compared to figures of primary level.

4.6. Public Expenditure on Education in India

In India over the last fifty years there have been major changes in the level of financing of education and in priorities attached to different sectors within it. Education at the primary level had been rather neglected by the early planners, who focused more on higher and technical education. The relative neglect of elementary education has resulted in low literacy rates among adults in India and in majority of the poor children remaining out-of-school, being deprived of even elementary education. Several commissions, committees, and policies were appointed after independence to deal with various issues in education. Many of them suggested higher investment in education and recommended expenditure of appropriate share of income of state and central government on education. In the post independent era the expenditure on education by the education department and other departments viz (i) Revenue Account, (ii) Capital Account and (iii) Loans and Advances as % of GDP is as follows:

Educational development in general and attainment of Universalisation of Elementary Education in particular, depends mostly on the expenditure on education. Kothari Commission (1964-66) recommended that public expenditure on education should reach the level of 6 percent of GDP by 1986. But we could not reach the said percentage as observed above. In the early decades after independence the government, for economic growth, emphasized on investment in the industrial sector. This among other is the reason for low percentage of expenditure on education till 1960-61. After recommendations of Kothari Commission (1964-66) to extend the public expenditure on education up to 6 percent of GDP, we can notice the incremental improvement in the budget expenditure on education over the next decades. The percentage of GDP expenditure on education in the year 2010-11was 4.05, which was very low compared to the expenditure of developed countries.

4.7 International Comparison of Public Expenditure on Education

Education is a key indicator for economic development of any country which is the reason why developed countries spend more share of their income on education. A country's wealth(defined as GDP per capita) is positively associated with expenditures per full-time-equivalent (FTE) student on education at the elementary and secondary level as well as at the post-secondary level. Report on '*Education at a Glance 2014*' of Organisation for Economic Cooperation and Development (OECD) declared the comparative figures on the expenditure on education. The OECD is an organisation of 34 countries whose purpose is to promote trade and economic growth. In the year 2011, the expenditure on education, of selected countries from OECD was as follows:

Among the OECD countries reporting data in 2011, five countries spent over 7 percent of their GDP on total education expenditures: Denmark (7.9 percent), Iceland (7.7 percent), the Republic of Korea (7.6 percent), New Zealand (7.5 percent), and Israel (7.3 percent). The United States spent just under 7 percent (6.9 percent) of its GDP on total education expenditures. The average expenditure on education as a percentage of GDP of the OECD countries was 6.1 percent, which was almost more than half of Indian expenditure.

Notes

1. Government of Maharashtra (1982), 'Babasaheb Ambedkar: Writings and Speeches', Vol. 2, p. 62.
2. Rao, G. Syamala (2012), 'Significance of Right to Education in India'. in Rao, Pulla (ed.), *Right to education as an Inclusive Policy*, New Delhi:ABD Publishers, pp. 112.
3. R. Govinda, Madhumita Bandyopadhyay (2008), *Access to Elementary Education in India,* Country analytical Review, New Delhi: NUEPA, pp. 4.
4. U-DISE - Elementary Education in India: Trends 2005-06 to 2014-15.
5. Rao, Syamala G. (2012), Significance of Right to Education, in Rao, Pulla (ed.) *Right to Education an Inclusive Policy*, ABD Publishers, New Delhi, p. 114.

Chapter - 5

Field Data Analysis

5.1 Educational Profile of the Selected Schools

The researcher visited 33 schools from the districts of Beed and Pune. Type of the schools, criteria for selection and reasoning for the same has been given earlier. In this topic the researcher has reviewed the educational and physical facilities of the selected school, teachers and students profile, pupil-teacher ratio and training for the teachers as per collected data etc.

(i) Educational and infrastructural facilities in the schools

Sections 19 and 25 of the RTE scheduled the norms and standards for schools. No school shall be established, or recognised unless it fulfills the norms and standards specified in the schedule. Where a school established before the commencement of this act does not fulfill the norms and standards specified in the schedule, it should take steps to fulfill such norms and standards at its own expenses, within a period of three years from the date of such commencement. On 1st April, 2013, India completed three years of the enactment of the RTE, 2009. The researcher tried to find the status of the educational and infrastructural facilities in the 33 selected schools for the study.

The researcher asked the headmaster, SMC members and students about availability of infrastructure facilities in the school. He personally crosschecked the actual status of the facilities by inspecting around the school. These facilities were regarding physical infrastructure and educational material. i.e. class rooms, separate toilets for boys and girls, safe drinking water, store room, playground, kitchen for mid-day meal and compound around the school. Most of the three category of the respondents gave positive responses about availability of physical infrastructure and academic material in the school.

Availability of facilities in the schools of Pune and Beed

(Digit in the brackets showing percentage and the question not asked indicated by --)

Facilities	Headmaster		SMC Member				Students	
	Yes	No	Yes	No	NR	Don't Know	Yes	No
(1) All-Weather-building	33 (100)	00 (00)	27 (96.43)	01 (3.57)	00 (00)	00 (00)	--	--
i. Separate class-room for every teacher	--	--	25 (89.29)	01 (3.57)	02 (7.14)	00 (00)	--	--
ii. Separate Office for Headmaster	33 (100)	00 (00)	22 (78.57)	04 (14.29)	02 (7.14)	00 (00)	--	--
iii. Separate Staff Room for teachers	--	--	23 (82.14)	03 (10.71)	02 (7.14)	00 (00)	--	--
iv. Store Room	--	--	24 (85.71)	02 (7.14)	02 (7.14)	00 (00)	--	--
v. Separate toilets for boys and girls	32 (96.97)	01 (3.03)	24 (82.71)	02 (7.14)	02 (7.14)	00 (00)	168 (85.28)	29 (14.72)
vi. Safe and adequate drinking water facility to all children	32 (96.97)	01 (3.03)	26 (92.86)	00 (00)	02 (7.14)	00 (00)	184 (93.40)	13 (6.60)
vii. Kitchen for mid-day meal	23 (69.70)	10 (30.30)	16 (57.14)	10 (35.71)	01 (3.57)	01 (3.57)	--	--
viii. Playground	27 (81.82)	06 (18.18)	21 (75)	05 (17.86)	02 (7.14)	00 (00)	175 (88.83)	22 (11.17)
ix. Compound to school	28 (84.85)	05 (15.15)	22 (78.57)	04 (14.29)	02 (7.14)	00 (00)	--	--
x. Ramp	22 (66.67)	11 (33.33)	--	--	--	00 (00)	--	--
(2) Teaching & learning equipment	--	--	20 (71.43)	02 (7.14)	03 (10.71)	03 (10.71)	--	--
(3) Library	27 (81.82)	06 (18.18)	24 (85.71)	02 (7.14)	02 (7.14)	00 (00)	--	--
i. Adequate books available in the library	27 (81.82)	**NA**- 6 (18.18)	17 (60.71)	08 (28.57)	02 (7.14)	01 (3.57)	--	--
ii. Register for book reciprocation in the library	--	--	16 (57.14)	08 (28.57)	03 (10.71)	01 (3.57)	--	--
(4) Play material games and sports equipment	--	--	21 (75)	05 (17.86)	02 (7.14)	00 (00)	170 (86.29)	04 (2.03) **Don't Know** 23 (11.68)

This data about availability of infrastructure facilities in the schools of Pune and Beed is formulated to check the ground realities. 100% of the headmasters said that they have all weather building while over 3% of the SMC members denied they had all weather building. Over 89% SMC members acknowledge availability of a separate class room for each teacher but over 3% noted the non-availability of the same. 100% headmasters had separate office but only over 78% SMC members acknowledged the availability of the same. Over 82% SMC members said that separate staff room were available for teachers while 10% SMC members said no separate staff room was available. Over 85% SMC members spoke about the availability of a store room and 7% said that it was not available. Regarding separate toilets for boys and girls over 96% headmasters spoke about the availability and 3% said separate toilets were not available. Among the SMC members over 82% said separate toilets were available and 7% acknowledge the absence. 85% students on being asked this question acknowledged the availability and 14% spoke about the non-availability of separate toilets. Over 96% headmasters said that safe and adequate drinking water facility was available for all children. While on the same issue 92% SMC members and 93% students acknowledged the same. Nearly 70% headmasters spoke about the availability of kitchen for mid-day meal and only 57% SMC members acknowledged the same. Over 81% headmasters, 75% SMC members and 88% students acknowledged the availability of a playground. Over 84% headmasters and 78% SMC members said that the school had a compound while only 66% headmasters acknowledged availability of a ramp for the physically challenged children.

Regarding the teaching and learning equipment over 71% SMC members acknowledged the availability. Regarding library and its availability over 81% headmasters and 85% SMC members acknowledged the same. And regarding adequacy of books in the library 81% headmasters and 60% SMC members acknowledge the adequacy. Regarding availability of register for the book reciprocation in the library only 57% SMC members accepted having the same. And finally 75% SMC members and 86% students responded positively to the availability of play material for games and sports equipment.

(ii) Teacher profile of the school

Teachers and students are the most important components of the school. Students are moulded by our teachers to be responsible citizen of the country. So the availability of full time, para and part-time teachers in Pune and Beed districts is in place. The number of teacher by their designation is as follows.

There were 632 teachers working in the surveyed schools. In all 91.46% teachers were fulltime, 6.80% teachers were working as a Para-teachers and 1.74% working as part-time teachers. All of the para and part-time teachers belonged to Pune district. The proportion of female teachers is significantly more than the male teachers in Pune district. The presence of higher number of women teachers in the schools of Pune district is an uplifting factor for the educational progress of the girl child and especially the girl child from a deprived social background.

(iii) Educational Qualification of Teachers

The RTE Act 2009 came in to force in April 2010 in India. Section 23 (1) and (2) are regarding the qualification for the appointment of the teacher. Minimum qualification for person to be eligible for appointment as a teacher for classes I to VIII is - Person with graduation with at least 50% marks and bachelor of Education (B. Ed) or at least 45% marks and one year of B.Ed in accordance with NCTE.In case of inadequacy of teacher education institutes or teachers possessing minimum qualification the central government may relax minimum qualification for a period not exceeding five years. Uttar Pradesh was given exemption from the above conditions of teacher appointment up to 31 March 2014. The relaxation conditions are as follows:

> (a) State government conduct TET. (b) State government and other school management amend recruitment rules regarding minimum qualification. (c) State government may give priority to eligible candidates with minimum qualification for appointment as teacher. (d) Advertisement of teacher appointment is published in and outside the state. (e) All appointed teachers undergo a six months special programme in elementary education. (f) No further extension of exemption. (g) State government should take steps to ensure qualified teacher recruitment. (The Gazette of India, Ministry of Human Resource Development (Department of School Education and Literacy), New Delhi, Notification, 10th September, 2012.)

The education of the selected teacher respondents are as follows:

The educational level of the teachers of selected schools is as follows. Most of the teachers were educated beyond minimum teacher qualification levels and well trained. In all 76.58% teachers were educated up to D.Ed/B.Ed and PG level. Five teachers completed M. Phil/Ph.D. 16.14% teachers were educated up to H.S.C level and teaching at the primary level. Five teachers were educated below SSC and teaching up to primary level. These teachers were retired but working in permanently non-grant school on lower remuneration. 5.70% teachers were educated up to SSC level and teaching up to the primary level.

In the district-wise scenario, the teachers who completed education up to degree/diploma and post-graduate levels is more in Pune than Beed district. Similarly in gender based qualifications female teachers were more educated than male teachers in Pune district.

(iv) Trained/Untrained Teachers

Teachers have to fulfill the minimum qualification as stated in section 23(1) and (2). Availability of trained teachers is the most important factor in successful implementation of the right to education in India. The number of trained and untrained teachers in Pune and Beed districts is as follows:

A teacher is considered to be trained teacher if he/she possesses a degree (B. Ed/B.Ped.) or diploma D.Ed. 98.26% of teachers from the selected schools completed these courses. Only 1.74% was found untrained, who did not possess those courses but were teaching up to the primary level. This was observed only in the non-grant schools from Pune district.

Even with the availability of abundant number of trained teachers, graduates or diploma holders, in Maharashtra, it is shocking to find even miniscule number of untrained teachers (1.74%).This phenomenon of non-availability of trained teachers is a big issue in states like Uttar Pradesh, Odisha and Jharkhand necessitating five year exemptions from the government for recruitment of trained teachers.

(v) In-service training completed by Teachers after 2008-09

A teacher has to perform some other duties in national interest, without allowing disturbance in his/herregular teaching. Along with this he/she has to participate in training programmes from time to time and participate in curriculum formulation and development of syllabi, training modules, textbook development and evaluations. With novelties under RTE such as continuous and comprehensive evaluation, creative learning aids for out of school children and children with special needs and recurring amendments in the RTE act necessitates teachers to know the new changes. Therefore, he/she have to undergo training in-service or before joining the service. The teachers from sampled schools completed the following training programmes after 2008-09 i.e. post RTE implementation.

Teacher training after 2008-09

Sr. No.	Response	Male-1		Female-2		Total
		Pune	Beed	Pune	Beed	
1.	Up to 1 week	26 (4.11)	74 (11.71)	91 (14.40)	53 (8.39)	244 (38.61)
2.	More than 1 week	37 (5.85)	49 (7.75)	66 (10.44)	19 (3.01)	171 (27.06)
3.	Teachers without in-service training	74 (11.71)	44 (6.96)	70 (11.08)	29 (4.59)	217 (34.33)
Total						**632 (100)**

The data reveals that, 415 (65.66%) teachers from the selected schools completed the in-service training. In Pune, 34.81% teachers completed in-service training. Of the teachers from Pune there were 18.51% teachers who completed training up to one week and 16.29% completed more than a weeks training programme. In Beed, there were 30.85% teachers who completed in-service training. Of the teachers from Beed there were 20.09% teachers who completed training up to one week and 10.76% teachers that completed more than a weeks training programme.

There were 34.33% teachers from both districts who did not receive any in-service training. These teacher included 22.79% from Pune and 11.55% from Beed district.

Regarding gender issues in the in-service training the above table reveals that, a better number of women teachers of Pune received in-service training compared to Beed and vice-versa better number of male teachers of Beed received in-service training as compared to Pune. This in a way reflects the significance given to female teacher for school education in a large city like Pune.

Even after so many years of the implementation of the RTE act it is surprising and disturbing that around 35% school teachers have not received any in-service training regarding RTE or otherwise. This could reflect poorly on the challenging teaching-learning process under the RTE. Furthermore, the SC or ST students are likely to be more vulnerable to be denied a simple and conducive learning process. It is also incidental that the schooling and other support systems have assisted the students from the schedule tribe or schedule caste to only average learning levels.

(vi) Total number of Students of selected schools

Student is the prime focus of the education system. Teachers and students are interrelated and the learning process depends on a healthy and dynamic relationship between the two. The student's profile of the selected schools is as follows:

The researcher visited 33 schools from Pune and Beed districts. Total numbers of students admitted in those schools were 17562, in which 10414(59.30%) were boys and 7148 (40.70%) were girl students. Number of students in Pune district is more than Beed as 18 schools in Pune were visited as compared to 15 from Beed.

(vii) Pupil-Teacher Ratio

The 25 (1) section of the RTE Act provides the guidelines of the pupil-teacher in a school. The specific pupil-teacher ratio for different levels of elementary education is given in the schedule of the norms and standards for a school in this act. As per this schedule the pupil-teacher ratio for first to fifth standards shall not exceed 40:1. For sixth to eighth standards it shall be 35:1. It means at least one teacher for 35 students.

As the data suggests, the pupil-teacher ratio for the first to fifth class of the selected schools is as follows - 42.42% school's pupil-teacher ratio is below 30, after that 27.27% school's pupil-teacher ratio was between 30 to 35. 12.12% schools' pupil-teacher ratio is above 40. Moreover, 12.12% respondents did not give any response for this question. It is evident that over 75% schools have maintained the correct pupil-teacher ratio i.e. 40:1 as required by the RTE.

According to the RTE the pupil-teacher ratio for the sixth to eighth standard shall be 35:1. It means at least one teacher for every thirty-five children. As the data shows, the pupil-teacher ratio of over 45% schools is below 30:1 which meant one teacher teaching thirty students in a class. 27.27% schools' Pupil-Teacher ratio was 30 to 35 and 21.21% schools' ratio was above 35. It means 7 schools out of 33 were not following the rules regarding pupil-teacher ratio for sixth to eight standard as stated in the RTE act.

Pupil-teacher ratio is a consideration of optimum communication workload that a teacher can handle in a classroom. It is matter of the reach of concentrated efforts of learning process between a teacher and a student. The more number of students the lower the impact of learning process between the two. As many as seven schools out of 33, even after six years of implementation of the RTE, could not get the pupil-teacher ratio right. This may be because of higher demand of admission for certain schools or schools saving on extra expenditure on teachers. As mentioned earlier the SC and ST students are more vulnerable to receive a diluted impact of the learning process in an overcrowded classroom.

5.2 Awareness about RTE

In India, a general perception reveals that the citizens are not very aware of their rights and obligations. Some Indian citizen, including people concerned with the school system, suffer from lack of awareness about the right to education act, which is one of the milestones in the Indian education system that came into force in April 2010. To know the general perception of the respondents about RTE Act awareness the researcher met teachers, SMC members, parents for their responses with interview schedule.

Do you know about the Act?

Respon-dents	Caste Category	Yes		No		Total
		Pune	Beed	Pune	Beed	
Teacher	Open	07 (18.92)	05 (13.51)	--	--	12 (32.43)
	S.C	01 (2.70)	01 (2.70)	--	--	02 (5.40)
	S.T	01 (2.70)	--	--	--	01 (2.70)
	OBC	03 (8.11)	03 (8.11)	--	--	06 (16.22)
	DNT	01 (2.70)	03 (8.11)	01 (2.70)	01 (2.70)	06 (16.22)
	Minority	08 (21.62)	02 (5.40)	--	--	10 (27.03)
Total		**21 (56.76)**	**14 (37.84)**	**01 (2.70)**	**01 (2.70)**	**37 (100)**

SMC	Open	04 (14.29)	03 (10.71)	02 (7.14)	--	09 (32.15)
	S.C	--	03 (10.71)	--	--	03 (10.71)
	S.T	01 (3.57)	--	01 (3.57)	--	02 (7.14)
	OBC	--	--	--	01 (3.57)	01 (3.57)
	DNT	--	02 (7.14)	--	01 (3.57)	03 (10.71)
	Minority	05 (17.86)	04 (14.29)	01 (3.57)	--	10 (35.72)
Total		**10 (35.71)**	**12 (42.86)**	**04 (14.29)**	**02 (7.14)**	**28 (100)**
Parents	Open	02 (7.14)	01 (3.57)	--	02 (7.14)	05 (17.86)
	S.C	02 (7.14)	--	--	03 (10.71)	05 (17.86)
	OBC	01 (3.57)	01 (3.57)	02 (7.14)	02 (7.14)	06 (21.42)
	DNT	01 (3.57)	--	01 (3.57)	03 (10.71)	05 (17.86)
	Minority	06 (21.43)	01 (3.57)	--	--	07 (25)
Total		**12 (42.86)**	**03 (10.71)**	**03 (10.71)**	**10 (35.72)**	**28 (100)**

As the data suggests, 94.60% teachers have information about the act, 5.40% teachers did not know about this act. Of the 94.60% teachers who have information about the RTE 56.76% were from Pune and 37.84% from Beed. Even after 6 years of the implementation of the RTE act it is astonishing to find that over 5% of teachers of the sample did not have information about the right to education act.

The teacher is the most vital cog in the successful implementation of the RTE act and even if a few teachers do not have information of the RTE act it raises serious doubts about the successful implementability of the RTE act. Furthermore, doubts could be raised about the reach of the positive implications of the RTE to the most vulnerable students of the school i.e. the once from the schedule castes and schedule tribes. This actually means that all school teachers have not been imparted training related to the RTE, which has been proven earlier. All teachers need to be imparted intensive training regarding all aspects of the RTE to enable passionate contribution from the teachers.

Regarding information of the RTE act with the members of the school management committee 78.57% members gave a positive response and 21.43% did not have any information. Of the 78.57% SMC members who have the information about RTE 35.71% respondents were from Pune district and 42.86% from Beed. But 14.29% members from Pune and 7.14% from Beed district did not have any information about the RTE act. It is clear that, the SMC members from Beed district are more aware compared to Pune district.

The RTE has, demonstrating classic democratic decentralisation, given legal authority to the school management committee for the constructive functioning of the school. As seen in the field data over 21 percent SMC members did not have any information about the RTE. Since community participation is of critical importance for the success of the RTE this rate of ignorance is undesirable. These 21% SMC members include 66% members from the socially deprived communities, whose active participation in the SMCs is of paramount importance for the prioritised consideration of the socially inclusive functioning of the RTE act.

Regarding parent's information about the RTE 53.57% parents were in the know while 46.53% did not have any information. As much as over 35% parents from Beed were found unaware about the act, while over 10.71% parents from Pune also were ignorant about the act.

Again parent's participation is significant for community participation in the implementation of the RTE act. Even in this case over 84% of the 36% parents were found ignorant of the act belonged to the deprived sections of the society. This clearly shows that even the basic information of the RTE has not reached the parents of the students from the most vulnerable sections of the society. Their informed participation is of crucial importance for their wards performance under the right of education in schooling.

It means after the fourth year of the implementation of this act a lot of persons were found unaware about this act. As observed in this study 22.58% respondents from the above mentioned three categories did not have information about the act.

5.3 Detailed opinion about the act

After the general opinion about the act, the researcher asked specifically teachers, SMC members and parents from the selected schools to give detailed opinion on the act. The respondents gave the following responses.

Detailed opinion about the RTE Act

Sr. No.	Detail Opinion	Teacher	SMC Member	Parents	Total
1.	Every child gets free andcompulsory education by this act	10 (27.03)	09 (32.14)	10 (35.71)	29 (31.18)
2.	RTE Act is very good for comprehensive development of the students, need positive co-operation from every one	14 (37.84)	07 (25)	03 (10.71)	24 (25.81)
3.	This act helps access to education for the disadvantaged section, it also helps to establish equality	04 (10.81)	01 (3.58)	00 (00)	05 (5.38)
4.	Non-detention and age-appropriate Admissions - these policies are good	03 (8.11)	02 (7.14)	02 (7.14)	07 (7.53)
5.	Attendance in the class has increased	01 (2.70)	00 (00)	00 (00)	01 (1.08)
6.	Irrelevant answer	02 (5.41)	00 (00)	00 (00)	02 (2.15)
7.	No Response	01 (2.70)	09 (32.14)	00 (00)	10 (10.75)
8.	Not Applicable	02 (5.41)	00 (00)	13 (46.43)	15 (16.12)
	Total	**37 (100)**	**28 (100)**	**28 (100)**	**93 (100)**

The data shows the detailed opinion of the respondents about the RTE act. 70.97% respondents from above three categories responded about the RTE act satisfactorily. 31.18% respondents replied that, all children get the right to free and compulsory education. 25.81% responded that RTE act was helpful for comprehensive development of the child. Only 5.68% respondents replied that education was accessible to all sections of the society by this act. 5.38% respondents thought the non-detention and age appropriate admission policy was good for the furtherance of education. Only one teacher said attendance of the students in class has increased by implementing free and compulsory education.

However, 10 (10.75%) respondents from above three categories have no information about act, as they did not answer this question.

Social Category of respondents who could not give details about RTE

Respondents	District	Social Category						
		Open	S.C	S.T	OBC	NT	Minority	Total
Teacher	Pune	00 (00)	00 (00)	00 (00)	00 (00)	00 (00)	02 (7.41)	02 (7.41)
	Beed	00 (00)	00 (00)	00 (00)	01 (3.70)	02 (7.41)	00 (00)	03 (11.11)
SMC Member	Pune	02 (7.41)	00 (00)	01 (3.70)	00 (00)	00 (00)	03 (11.11)	06 (22.22)
	Beed	00 (00)	00 (00)	00 (00)	01 (3.70)	01 (3.70)	01 (3.70)	03 (11.11)
Parents	Pune	00 (00)	00 (00)	00 (00)	02 (7.41)	01 (3.70)	00 (00)	03 (11.11)
	Beed	02 (7.41)	03 (11.11)	00 (00)	02 (7.41)	00 (00)	03 (11.11)	10 (37.04)
Total		**04 (14.82)**	**03 (11.11)**	**01 (3.70)**	**06 (22.22)**	**04 (14.82)**	**09 (33.33)**	**27 (100)**

It is extremely worrying that 18.52% teachers, 33.33% SMC member and 48.15% parents did not know any details of the RTE act. Of the 18.52% teachers 11.11% did not respond to the question and 7.41% did not give a relevant answer.

Teacher is the most important unit of the education system. He/she is responsible for the successful implementation of this act; if he/she is not aware about the details of the act then achieving the goal of universal education will be a difficult process. Parents that are not aware of the details of the RTE shall also not help the cause of their children's education. Furthermore among the 13 parents who could not give details about the RTE over 3 were from schedule caste, over 4 were from the other backward classes and one from the nomadic tribes and 3 were from the minorities. And among the 9 SMC members one was from the scheduled tribes, one from the OBC, one from the nomadic tribes and four from the minorities. It is evident that ignorance of details of the right to education is highly prevalent among the deprived communities of the society. This calls for better efforts of dissemination of information of the RTE with a dynamic and inclusive functioning and implementation of the right to education act.

5.4. Admission process of the school and RTE Act

Right to education act 2009 provides the right to free education to every child of the age six to fourteen years in India. Wherever a child wants admission in a neighbourhood school, he/she has the right to get admission in that school. Screening test of the child or his parents or guardian for admission of the child in elementary education is prohibited and punishable by section 13(1) b.

(i) Age limit for the admission under RTE

Section 3 of the RTE act provides to every child of the age of six to fourteen years the right to free and compulsory education in a neighbourhood school till the completion of elementary education. However, in India the elementary education starts with the age of 2 and half years. The schools take the kids in pre-nursery if they are three years of age. A child who has an early schooling since the age of 3 will be far ahead from the child who enters the school at the age of 6.The ability of participation of SC and ST students in pre-primary schooling is extremely unlikely, especially in rural and remote areas due to socio-economic obstacles. Other students get an opportunity to participate in pre-primary education, giving them a head start to tackle proper schooling. Therefore, the act does not take care of the children aged below six. The maximum limit of 14 years for free and compulsory education is also a hindrance to the entrance of SC and ST students to further and higher education. At age 14 a student passes only 8th standard and with the no-detention policy in place, pushing forward students without prescribed learning levels, the likelihood of the child going on to secondary and later higher education is quite low. So the upper age limit should be extended to sixteen years i.e. 10 standard. This will increase chances of backward class students' entrance in to the domain of higher education.

The age group for free and compulsory education should be 3 to 16 under RTE. Even Sri Lanka, a neighbourhood developing country has provision of free and compulsory education to children between 5 and 14 years of age.

Even the RTE act of Finland provides for pre-primary education which is a year preceding compulsory schooling, voluntary additional basic education for those who have completed the basic education syllabus for instruction preparing immigrants for basic education and for before and after school activities.

(ii) Screening Test

Section 13 provides that no school or person shall collect capitation fee or subject a child to any screening procedure. The government issued the guidelines under the section 35(1) i.e. schools adopt an admission procedure that is non-discriminatory, rational and transparent, and that schools do not subject children and their parents to admission tests and interview in order to decide whether they will admit a child or not.

The researcher reviewed the admission process of the surveyed schools. The researcher asked about the screening test for admission to the headmasters, students and parents. The responses were as follows:

> 18.18% headmasters, 34.01% students and 32.14% parents said that screening test of the students have been taken by the school for admission. This is a clear violation of the section 13 clause 2 (b) of the RTE act which strictly prohibits screening test of the students for admission. A fine, as penalty has also been provided for by the act against schools that violate this provision. 60% respondents stated that their admission policy did not involve any screening process.

Conducting screening tests in a number of schools for admission, besides being illegal, clearly defeats the very purpose of equality of opportunities and challenge to quality performance of schools that is sought to be achieved under the RTE act. The school authorities act of checking out the socio-economic, financial and educational antecedents of the child and his parents goes against the most vulnerable students who come from the SC, ST communities. They incidentally happen to be first and second generation learners that do not need admission obstacles such as a screening test.

(iii) Documents required for admission in Elementary Education

Documents are acceptable as age proof for purpose of admission according to section 14 (1) of the RTE - (a) Birth certificate under registration of Birth and Deaths Act, 1969 or (b) Register or record maintained by the hospital or auxiliary nurse and midwife in respect of the birth place of the child. (c) Anganwadi record. (d) In case the record of date of birth is not available a declaration by parents of the child stating the date of birth is to be held valid. (e) In case of a child belonging to disadvantaged group or weaker section, declaration of the age of the child by the parents or guardian, certified by the Sarpanch of the village or Head Master of the local school, or in case of urban or semi-urban area, by an office notified by the Government in that behalf is to be held valid. Even if a child does not hold any of the above mentioned documents he/she cannot be denied admission by any school. Headmaster of the surveyed schools were asked about the documents they requisitioned for admission at primary level.

Documents for admission asked for by the school - Headmaster

Sr. No.	Types of Documents	Pune	Beed	Total	Percent
1.	Birth certificate	01	04	05	15.15
2.	Migration Certificate	00	03	03	9.09
3.	Caste Certificate	00	00	00	0.00
4.	Transfer Certificate	02	02	04	12.12
5.	All the above	02	03	05	15.15
6.	None of these	01	00	01	3.04
7.	Birth & Migration Certificate	02	00	02	6.06
8.	Birth certificate, Migration Certificate, Caste Certificate	02	02	04	12.12
9.	Birth certificate, Caste Certificate	03	00	03	9.09
10.	Birth certificate, Caste Certificate, Transfer Certificate	01	01	02	6.06
11.	Birth certificate, Transfer Certificate	02	00	02	6.06
12.	Admission even if none of the documents available	01	01	02	6.06
Total		**18**	**15**	**33**	**100.00**

As seen in the data, over 15% schools asked for birth certificate as proof of age for admission. 12.12% headmasters said transfer certificate is necessary if the child has come from other school. 9.09% respondents said migration certificate is essential and 15.15%

respondents said proof of age, transfer certificate, caste certificate and migration certificate is necessary. Moreover, over 93% schools asked for one or the other documents for admission in the school. Only two school headmasters knew about the RTE provision of granting admission even when no documents were available with the child/ parent.

The admission process under RTE necessitates submission of documents as proof of age or academic credentials but even then the RTE, in pursuit of universalisation of education, has also mandated grant of admissions to those students/parents who do not have any essential documents.

This extraordinary exemption, on documents for admission, is extremely praiseworthy as students coming from the schedule caste, schedule tribe, the de-notified or nomadic tribes come from backgrounds where producing necessary documents could be a very difficult proposition due to rootlessness or migratory necessities or lack of access to proper health or educational systems. But the fact that only two of the surveyed headmasters were aware of the process of admission even without necessary documents is disturbing. This shows the lack of knowledge of even the basics with the headmasters who lead the school system. Awareness of this exemption not only with the headmaster but with all other functionaries of the school is vital for the inclusion of children from the SC, ST and other deprived communities.

(iv) Charges/Capitation fees for admission

Charging capitation fee for admission of a child in elementary education has been prohibited by section 13(1) of the RTE act. Many eligible students from socio-economic backward communities like the SC and ST are denied entrance in to 'so called' better unaided schools due to capitation fee, deposits or other such charges. No child shall be liable to pay any kind of fee, charges, or expenses, which may prevent him or her from pursuing and completing the elementary education. The researcher also found out the different types of fees that could be charged for admission.

Management-wise schools which taken fees

Sr. No.	Management of School	Fees							Total
		Admission fee	Exam Fee	Traveling	Computer	Consolidated	Admission and Exam fees	None	
1.	Tribal Department	00 (00)	00 (00)	00 (00)	02 (6.06)	00 (00)	00 (00)	01 (3.03)	**03 (9.09)**
2.	Z.P.	00 (00)	00 (00)	00 (00)	00 (00)	00 (00)	00 (00)	04 (12.12)	**04 (12.12)**
3.	Municipal Corporation	00 (00)	00 (00)	00 (00)	00 (00)	00 (00)	01 (3.03)	01 (3.03)	**02 (6.06)**
4.	Nagar Palika	00 (00)	00 (00)	00 (00)	00 (00)	00 (00)	00 (00)	01 (3.03)	**01 (3.03)**
5.	Private-Aided	01 (3.03)	03 (9.09)	01 (3.03)	00 (00)	00 (00)	00 (00)	08 (24.24)	**13 (39.39)**
6.	Private-Un Aided	02 (6.06)	01 (3.03)	00 (00)	00 (00)	03 (9.09)	00 (00)	03 (9.09)	**09 (27.27)**
7.	Poona cantonment board	00 (00)	00 (00)	00 (00)	00 (00)	00 (00)	00 (00)	01 (3.03)	**01 (3.03)**
	Total	**03 (9.09)**	**04 (12.12)**	**01 (3.03)**	**02 (6.06)**	**03 (9.09)**	**01 (3.03)**	**19 (57.58)**	**33 (100)**

As evident from the above table over 15% private aided schools charged one or the other fees to students which included one school charging admission fee another charging for travel to school and three schools collecting exam fees. This is a gross violation of the right to free education between six to fourteen years as section 2 (n) (ii) of the RTE act provides for free education in unaided schools receiving aid or grant to meet whole or part of its expenses from the appropriate government or the local authority. This willful breach of law by private aided schools exposes the students from vulnerable communities such as the SC and ST to dropping out of schooling.

The data also shows over 19% private unaided schools charged fees up to upper primary level which included two schools charging admission fees, one school charging exam fees and three schools charging the whole consolidated fees. This also is a gross violation of the right to free education and exposes the profiteering tendencies of the un-aided schools along with their reluctance to accommodate 25% disadvantaged and weaker section students from the neighborhood even when state reimbursement of the expenses of the 25% quota students is legally provided for. Surprisingly one Municipal Corporation school has charged for admission and exam fees in total violation of the act. This highlights complete ignorance on the part of government schools that need to be well informed and trained for successful implementation of the RTE. While the tribal department, Zilla Parishad, Nagarpalika and Poona cantonment board schools have all followed the fundamentals provisions of the RTE, by not charging any fees whatsoever.

5.5 Admission process under 25% reservation quota

The most important provision in this act is the provision for admissions under 25% reservation quota. Section 12 of the Right of Children to Free and Compulsory Education Act 2009 has made it compulsory for every private unaided school to admit at least 25% of its admission to the entry level class from children belonging to the disadvantaged and weaker section groups (DWS). For this category of students the state government will reimburse to the unaided schools an amount equal to either the fees charged by the school or the per child expenditure in state schools, whichever is lower.

Section 2(d) defines a disadvantaged group as a group in which a child belongs to the Scheduled Caste (SC), the Scheduled Tribe (ST), the socially and educationally backward class or such other group having disadvantage owing to social, cultural, economical, geographical, linguistic, gender or such other factor, as may be specified by the appropriate Government considered as a disadvantaged group. Moreover, sub section (e) of section 2, "child belonging to weaker section" means a child belonging to the parent or guardian whose annual income is lower than the limit specified by the appropriate government.

Most of the private unaided schools are opposing the admission under 25% reservations quota due to the defective government reimbursement system. For effective implementation of the 25% seats in private schools, there is a need to ensure a fair selection process, adequate and timely reimbursement from the state and a transparent monitoring and evaluation system.The researcher investigated the implementation of admissions under this provision with the headmasters, teachers, parents, SMC members and students.

(i) Opinion about 25% reservation quota

Proper implementation of the 25% reservation quota totally depends on the positive attitude of the school towards neighbourhood students who come from the disadvantaged and weaker sections of the society. The researcher traced the attitudes of the teacher and SMC members about the 25% reservation quota provisions as follows:

Teachers' opinion about 25% reservations Quota

Sr.No	Response	Open	SC	ST	OBC	NT	Minority	Total
1.	This policy would be helpful to establishing equality in the society.	01 (2.70)	00 (00)	00 (00)	01 (2.70)	00 (00)	01 (2.70)	03 (8.11)
2.	Students from economically backward section getting opportunities to take education & helpful for comprehensive development.	02 (5.41)	01 (2.70)	00 (00)	00 (00)	00 (00)	00 (00)	03 (8.11)
3.	This policy is too good need proper implementation	00 (00)	00 (00)	00 (00)	02 (5.41)	01 (2.70)	03 (8.11)	06 (16.22)
4.	This policy is not good	00 (00)	00 (00)	00 (00)	01 (2.70)	00 (00)	00 (00)	01 (2.70)
5.	No response	09 (24.32)	01 (2.70)	01 (2.70)	02 (5.41)	05 (13.51)	06 (16.22)	24 (64.86)
Total		**12 (32.43)**	**02 (5.41)**	**01 (2.70)**	**06 (16.22)**	**06 (16.22)**	**10 (27.02)**	**37 (100)**

Teacher's opinion about the 25% reservation quota is an important indicator of the teachers outlook towards accommodating participation of the students from the socio-economically deprived communities into the mainstream education system. As much as 65% of the teachers did not respond to this query. Representing sheer indifference or disdain for this admission provision. Around 3% teachers felt this policy to be no good, meaning to be interpreted as not serving the best academic interests of the disadvantaged and weaker sections students or resistance on their educational participation in the elite unaided private schools. Over 8% teachers thought this provision to be helpful to establish equality in the society and a similar percentage thought this provision creating educational opportunities for the disadvantaged and weaker section students. Significant 60% teachers thought this policy to be very good that needed proper implementation.

The majority of the responses from the teachers towards this provision was either of neglect or negation which expose the teacher's attitude towards this policy which expressly claims the opportunity of quality education participation to the DWS of the neighbourhood. This indicates maladministration of a significant socially inclusive policy of the RTE.

While understanding the SMC member's opinion about the 25% neighbourhood admissions quota we realise that only over 21% members supported the idea of admissions for the students from disadvantaged and weaker sections from the neighbourhood. Incidentally, again over 3% SMC members noted that their schools were not interested for such neighbourhood admissions. And a huge over 53% SMC members simply did not respond to the query on the 25% admissions quota for the deprived students of their neighbourhood. It is extremely unfortunate that members of the school management committee, which got a statutory role in the functioning of the school system under the RTE, are either negligent or unsupportive for the participation of students from the socially and economically underprivileged sections. Incidentally, the disadvantage groups under this quota include the students from the scheduled castes and scheduled tribes. This negative opinion or stance of the SMC members empowered through democratic decentralisation highlights the age-old tendencies of social distance and alienation alive though with a tempered down intensity. The issue of awareness and sensitisation of the SMC members towards the educational participation of the students from the disadvantaged and weaker sections needs to be addressed. This can be achieved only through consistence and intense SMC member's training/workshop through government agencies and credible NGOs.

(ii) Documents submitted at the time of admission in 25% reservation Quota

Documents are acceptable as age proof for purpose of section 14 (1) which is regarding proof of age for admission- (a) Birth certificate under registration of Birth and Death Act, 1969. or (b) Register or record maintained by the hospital or auxiliary nurse and midwife in respect of the birth place of the child. (c) Anganwadi record. (d) In case the record is not available a declaration by parents of the child stating the date of birth. (e) In case of a child belonging to disadvantaged group or weaker section, declaration of the age of the child by the parents or guardian, certified by the Sarpanch of the village or Head Master of the local school, or in case of urban or semi-urban area, by an office notified by the Government in that behalf. A child who does not possess above-mentioned documents should not be denied admission by any school. Under the survey, the parents who sought admission under reservation policy submitted the following documents.

Documents submitted at time of admission by parents

Sr. No.	Response	Pune	Beed	Total	Percent
1.	Income Certificate issued by Revenue officer	01	00	01	3.57
2.	Caste Certificate for SC/ST/ OBC/VJNT/SBC	00	01	01	3.57
3.	Residential proof	00	01	01	3.57
4.	All of above	01	00	01	3.57
5.	None of the above	00	00	00	0.00
6.	Form No. 2, Caste Cert& proof of Resident	00	01	01	3.57
7.	Not Applicable	13	10	23	82.15
Total		**15**	**13**	**28**	**100.00**

The schools under the survey can and do demand for documents regarding income, social category and residential proof for admission under the 25% reservation quota. Even then, the RTE mandates all eligible schools to give admission to the students from the disadvantaged and weaker sections even if they did not possess any of the necessary documents for admission. Over 3% parents submitted the income certificate, social category certificates, residential proof and the combination of the caste certificates and proof of residence for admission under the 25% neighbourhood reservation quota.

(iii) Admission Denied by the schools under 25% quota

School cannot deny the admission to any child for not having any document or proof of age; because section 14(2) assured that, no child shall be denied admission in a school for lack of age proof.

Admissions denied by school- Parents

Sr. No	Response	Open	S.C	OBC	NT	Minority	Total
1.	Yes	00 (00)	01 (3.57)	00 (00)	00 (00)	01 (3.57)	**02 (7.14)**
2.	No	04 (14.29)	03 (10.71)	05 (17.86)	02 (7.14)	09 (32.14)	**23 (82.14)**
3.	No response	01 (3.57)	01 (3.57)	01 (3.57)	00 (00)	00 (00)	**03 (10.71)**
Total		**05 (17.86)**	**05 (17.86)**	**06 (21.43)**	**02 (7.14)**	**10 (35.71)**	**28 (100)**

It is observed that over 7% parents acknowledged that the schools they approached before this one denied admission to their wards. Over 82% parents were not denied admission which may fall under the open seat quota or the 25% quota. The following data underlines the reasons for admissions denied under the 25% quota.

Reasons for denying the admissions – Parents

Sr. No.	Reasons for denying admission	Pune	Beed	Total
1.	Parents were uneducated, not having English knowledge	02 (7.14)	00 (00)	**02 (7.14)**
2.	No response	00 (00)	02 (7.14)	**02 (7.14)**
3.	Not applicable	13 (46.43)	11 (39.29)	**24 (85.72)**
Total		**15 (53.57)**	**13 (46.43)**	**28 (100)**

Over 7% parents stated that the schools with English medium of education denied their ward admission because they were either uneducated or did not know English. Under the RTE neither denial for admission for any reason nor conducting any screening test is permitted. This is a gross violation of the rights of education especially of the children from the SC and ST categories whose parents incidentally could be uneducated or lacked in English language skills underlined by the much lower literacy rates of the SC and ST in India.

(iv) Notification about 25% admissions by school

Government should post a notification in local newspapers as well as through speaker announcements on the community radio and local cable TV channels to build awareness of the rights of disadvantaged groups and weaker sections to seek admissions in private schools. Along with this each school should announce the number of seats reserved under the Act on their school website and front gate notice board, besides providing information of available number of seats to the state/local authority. The researcher asked the headmaster, teacher and SMC members about the advertisement of 25% reservation seats and got the following responses :

The researcher crosschecked the responses of headmasters, teachers and SMC members. Among the respondents 27.78% headmasters from Pune and 26.67% respondents from Beed gave positive responses. But most of the teachers, and SMC members gave negative responses. 54.55% teachers from Pune and 85.71% from Beed district said their schools did not publish the advertisement for the 25% reservation.

Overall most of respondents gave negative responses for this question. 17.39% said that the policy of 25% reservation was not applicable to their school and 15.22% respondents did not give any response for the same, 10(71.43%) SMC members from Beed district did not give any response. It means that only 22.83% respondents said the school published the advertisement of the 25% reservation quota. An overwhelming 44% of the headmasters, teachers, and SMC members acknowledged that they did not publicise the admissions available under the 25% quota. Such overwhelming numbers of denial of publicity to the 25% quota amounts to the gross violation of the right to free and compulsory education of the disadvantaged groups and weaker section which includes the students from the scheduled castes and scheduled tribes.

(v) Place of the advertisement for 25% quota

The notification about the details of 25% reservation quotas should be placed in the newspaper or on the school's website and notice board or in Grampanchayat office. The researcher tried to find out the place of advertisement about the 25% reservation in surveyed schools and the responses are as follows –

As observed from the above table only one headmaster and one teacher from Pune district said that the advertisement was placed in the local newspaper. 22.22% headmasters, 18.18% teachers and 22.22% SMC members from Pune district and only one headmaster from Beed district said the advertisement were placed on the notice board of their schools. Two headmasters from Pune district said it was published in the local newspaper and put on the school notice board.

It is clearly seen from the above table that besides over 44% schools that did not publish the 25% quota in any manner, those who have published the same have done it through only one or two publishing avenues. This is a way of concealing available 25% quota seats for the disadvantaged and the weaker sections of the neighbourhood, which includes the SC and ST children. This also reveals the overwhelming desire of non-accommodation of the unaided schools towards the deprived neighbourhood students and incompetence on the part of aided schools regarding accommodation of SC, ST and poor students in to schooling.

(vi) Number of admission and vacant seats under 25% reservation quota in schools

The researcher noticed the lack of awareness about the admission under the 25% reservation quota in all the schools. The researcher asked the headmaster and teachers about number of admissions and vacant seats under 25% reservation quota in the current academic year. Twenty-one (63.64%) headmasters did not give any responses which included 11 headmasters from Pune and 10 from Beed district. Further, the researcher asked about the vacant seats under the reservation quota and over 15% headmasters acknowledged having vacancies under the 25% quota. And over 84% headmasters did not respond to this query.

Researcher asked the headmasters about the number of admissions done under the 25% reservation quota. 61.11% headmasters from Pune did not give any response and of 6 unaided private schools from Pune 50% schools gave admission to 58 students from the disadvantaged and weaker sections under the 25% reservation quota. While in Beed none of the headmaster gave any response to the issue of 25% quota admission. Here all three unaided schools did not report any admissions under the 25% reservation quota.

It is very clear from the above data that the admissions under the 25% reservation quota for the neighbourhood backward and poor students are not well implemented.

(vii) Extra application received under 25% reservation quota

As response to school's advertisement regarding 25% reserved admission in class one of the school, applications may exceed over the available number of seats. In such a condition the school have to follow the guidelines formulated by the government. The researcher asked the headmasters and the SMC members about received applications under the reservation quota and the responses were as follows:

Of the headmasters and SMC members 67.86% did not give any response to this question. Only five (15.15%) headmasters from Beed district acknowledged that they received extra applications than available seats under the 25% quota. 9 (50%) headmasters from Pune and 17.39% SMC members from both districts gave negative responses. It means few schools received extra applications for the admission under 25% reservation quota. This reveals the sheer lack of publicity on the part of schools and government agencies regarding availability of seats under the 25% quota. This severely hurts the education opportunities of the slum children and the children residing in remote areas.

(viii) Criteria used for admission if additional application received were more than available seats

In case the number of applications for admission against the free seats at entry level class exceeds the number of free seats available, admission shall be made by draw of lots in the presence of at least three members as follows- one of whom shall be a representative of the parents and teacher association; one nominee of the management of the school; and nominee of the education officer. Five headmasters acknowledged that their school received extra applications. The criteria used for such admission by the schools is as follow:

It is surprising that no school made the admissions by draw of lots as stated in the notification regarding the 25% reservation seats. Only one SMC member from Beed district said that their admissions were made on the income criteria of the children and another said their school gave the admission on the criteria of first come first basis.

Three headmasters from Pune district said their school did not use any criteria for the admission in such conditions. Two SMC members said the admissions given to students as directed by Zilla Parishad.

As a solution to schools not following the process of drawing of lots for admissions under 25% quota if excess applications are received, the state government has centralised the whole admission process of the 25% quota admissions avoiding the indiscretions of errant unaided private schools.

(ix) School's actions if fewer applications received than available seats

In case the number of applications for admission against the free seats is below the number of seats available, admission shall be given to the available applicants and the vacant seats shall be re-notified for inviting further applications by following a similar procedure. The action of the school and school management committee is as follows:

School's Action if fewer Applications received

Sr. No.	Response	Pune		Beed		Total	
		Head-master	SMC Member	Head-master	SMC Member	Head-master	SMC Member
1.	Re-advertise for the vacant seats	01 (5.56)	00 (00)	00 (00)	00 (00)	01 (5.56)	00 (00)
2.	Vacant seats opened for general admis-sion process	01 (5.56)	00 (00)	02 (13.33)	00 (00)	03 (9.09)	00 (00)
3.	Did not process	01 (5.56)	00 (00)	02 (13.33)	01 (7.14)	03 (9.09)	01 (4.35)
4.	No Response	00 (00)	04 (44.44)	00 (00)	13 (92.86)	00 (00)	17 (73.91)
5.	Not applicable	15 (83.33)	05 (55.56)	11 (73.34)	00 (00)	26 (78.79)	05 (21.74)
	Total	**18 (100)**	**09 (100)**	**15 (100)**	**14 (100)**	**33 (100)**	**23 (100)**

73.91% SMC members did not give any response to this question. Only one headmaster from Pune district said the school re-published the advertisement of vacant seats under reservation quota, one SMC member and 3(9.09%) headmasters replied that their schools did not proceed to fulfill the vacant seats. Moreover, three (9.09%) headmasters said the vacant seats were declared open for unreserved admission. It means most of the schools did not process for re-advertisement to fill the vacant seats under 25% reservation quota. This again amounts to denial of admission to the SC and ST students from the disadvantaged groups and weaker sections that were left out of the first round of admission under the 25% quota due to lack of information, illiteracy etc.

(x) Criteria used for admission on 25% reservation Quota

Every school shall reserve the seats for admission, to at least twenty five percent of its strength of the class one of the school, for the child belonging to weaker section and the disadvantaged groups. Child belonging to disadvantaged groups means child belonging to SC and ST and any other category as is specified to be a group by the state government. As well as weaker sections means child belonging to the VJNT, OBC, SBC and the religious minorities by the government and those children whose parents or guardians annual income is lower than the minimum limit specified by the appropriate government, by notification. It means the school has to give admission to the above specified students and preference shall be given to the girl child. In the surveyed school the criteria used by the school for the admission under 25% reservation quota was follows:

As is seen from the data over 12% headmasters, one SMC member considered and one parent said that annual income of the parents was criteria for the admission in 25% reservation quota. Only one headmaster said that the school considered the social category i.e. SC or ST, concurred by over 14% parents who considered as criteria for 25% quota admission. While over 15% headmasters said that they gave the admissions on the below poverty line criteria.

Surprisingly 69.70% headmasters said the twenty-five percent reservations was not applicable to their school. This was because they need not have any admission quota because they were public or private aided schools. Moreover, 69.56% SMC members did not give any response out of neglect for these quota admission or their schools did not have any admission under the 25% quota.

Criteria for admission on 25% reserved seats

Sr. No.	Response	Pune			Beed			Total		
		Head-master	SMC Member	Parents	Head-master	SMC Member	Parents	Head-master	SMC Member	Parents
1.	Annual Income of parents	01 (5.56)	00 (00)	00 (00)	03 (20)	01 (7.14)	01 (7.69)	04 (12.12)	01 (4.35)	01 (30.57)
2.	Candidates from SC/ST	01 (5.56)	00 (00)	02 (13.33)	00 (00)	00 (00)	02 (15.38)	01 (3.03)	00 (00)	04 (14.29)
3.	Below poverty line cert & caste category	04 (22.22)	00 (00)	00 (00)	01 (6.67)	00 (00)	00 (00)	05 (15.15)	00 (00)	00 (00)
4.	Students allocated from ZP	00 (00)	02 (22.22)	00 (00)	00 (00)	01 (7.14)	00 (00)	00 (00)	03 (13.04)	00 (00)
5.	Not applicable	12 (66.67)	03 (33.33)	13 (86.67)	11 (73.33)	00 (00)	10	23 (69.70)	03 (13.04)	23 (82.14)
6.	No Response	00 (00)	04 (44.45)	00 (00)	00 (00)	12 (85.71)	00 (00)	00 (00)	16 (69.56)	00 (00)
	Total	**18 (100)**	**09 (100)**	**15 (100)**	**15 (100)**	**14 (100)**	**13 (100)**	**33 (100)**	**23 (100)**	**28 (100)**

(xi) Parent awareness about the 25% reservation

Children of the parents from the disadvantaged groups come under the 25% reservation policy, but information about the reservation quota does not reach such parents due to lack of awareness and low literacy levels. The researcher asked parents about the twenty-five percent reservation policy. Do they know about it?

Do You Know about the 25% admission quota - Parents

Sr. No	Response	Open	S.C	OBC	NT	Minority	Total
1.	Yes	02 (7.14)	03 (10.71)	02 (7.14)	00 (00)	04 (14.29)	**11 (39.29)**
2.	No	02 (7.14)	02 (7.14)	04 (14.29)	01 (3.57)	06 (21.43)	**15 (53.57)**
3.	No response	01 (3.57)	00 (00)	00 (00)	01 (3.57)	00 (00)	**02 (7.14)**
Total		**05 (17.86)**	**05 (17.86)**	**06 (21.43)**	**02 (7.14)**	**10 (35.71)**	**28 (100)**

The data clearly shows that the majority of the parents i.e. over 53% which includes 7% SC, 14% OBC, 3% NT and 21% minority parents did not have the information about the 25% reservation quota policy. Only 39.29% parents had the information about the 25% reservation quota admission policy. This situation warrants organisation of awareness programmes and publication of the 25% admission quota facility in the rural as well as urban areas.

(xii) Children admitted under 25% reservation quota

Focus of this study is to find out the social inclusion in the elementary education through the implementation of right to education act 2009. The researcher has purposely tried to interact with the parents from disadvantaged groups. Most of the schools were unwilling about filling reservation seats, so we could interact with only a limited number of parents from disadvantaged groups. The researcher tried to know the situation of admissions under 25% reservation quota and the responses are as follows:

Admission under 25% reservation quota - parents

Sr. No.	Response	Pune	Beed	Total	Percent
1.	Yes	01	01	02	7.14
2.	No	13	10	23	82.14
3.	No Response	01	02	03	10.71
	Total	**15**	**23**	**28**	**100.00**

Only two parents, one from each district said they had got the admissions for their children under 25% reservation quota, 3(10.71%) did not give any response and 82.14% parent respondents gave a negative response.

This clearly shows that very few parents from the disadvantaged groups and weaker sections could access the 25% admission reservation quota. This could be due to lack of awareness of the quota or that the parents from these sections were confronted with obstacles to access this quota. This clearly leads to exclusion of the SC, ST students from the right of free education.

(xiii) Efforts taken by parents for admission under 25% reservation quota

To get admission in the private unaided schools the parents have to take extra efforts. Parents from disadvantaged sections faced a lot of problems in accessing the 25% reservation quota admission due to the un-accommodative approach of the school. So they either have to apply to more than one school or take the help of local renowned persons for admissions. The researcher asked the parents about their efforts for admission under this policy and the responses are as follows –

Efforts taken by parents for admission in better private school

Sr. No	Response	Open	S.C	OBC	NT	Minority	Total
1.	Applied for admission in more than one school.	01 (3.57)	00 (00)	01 (3.57)	00 (00)	00 (00)	**02** **(7.14)**
2.	Took the help of the member of Local self-government	00 (00)	00 (00)	00 (00)	00 (00)	00 (00)	**00** **(00)**
3.	Give the donation for Admission	00 (00)	00 (00)	01 (3.57)	00 (00)	01 (3.57)	**02** **(7.14)**
4.	No response	00 (00)	00 (00)	00 (00)	00 (00)	01 (3.57)	**01** **(3.57)**
5.	Not Applicable	04 (14.29)	05 (17.86)	04 (14.29)	02 (7.14)	08 (28.57)	**23** **(82.15)**
	Total	**05** **(17.86)**	**05** **(17.86)**	**06** **(21.43)**	**02** **(7.14)**	**10** **(35.71)**	**28** **(100)**

Only two parents said they had got the admission for their children under the 25% reservation quota policy without taking any extra efforts. Over 7% parents admitted to have given donation for school admission under the 25% reservation quota. School demanding donations for admission is a clear infringement of the right to education act and socially exclusionary act against the students from the disadvantaged groups and weaker sections such incidents warrants locally centralised admissions and effective monitoring of the 25% quota admissions.

(xiv) Government reimbursement for the admissions under 25% reservation quota

Section 12 (2) of the RTE act specified the reimbursement process for the private unaided school. The private unaided school shall be reimbursed expenditure as incurred by it to the extent of per-child expenditure incurred by the state, or the actual amount charged from the child, whichever is lower. The reimbursement process was queried with the headmaster and SMC members with responses as follows:

Reimbursement from the Government

Sr. No.	Response	Pune		Beed		Total	
		Head-master	SMC Member	Head-master	SMC Member	Head-master	SMC Member
1.	Amount not received from the government	11 (33.33)	00 (00)	14 (42.42)	01 (3.57)	25 (75.76)	01 (3.57)
2.	As per government rules	05 (15.15)	00 (00)	01 (3.03)	00 (00)	06 (18.18)	00 (00)
3.	Don't Know	00 (00)	00 (00)	00 (00)	01 (3.57)	00 (00)	01 (3.57)
4.	Not Applicable	02 (6.06)	06 (21.43)	00 (00)	00 (00)	02 (6.06)	06 (21.43)
5.	No Response	00 (00)	08 (28.57)	00 (00)	12 (42.86)	00 (00)	20 (71.43)
Total		**18 (54.54)**	**14 (50)**	**15 (45.46)**	**14 (50)**	**33 (100)**	**28 (100)**

A whopping over 75% headmaster and one SMC member said that they did not receive any amount from the government as reimbursement for admission done under the 25% reservation quota. Only 18.18% headmasters said that their schools received reimbursement amount as per government norms. It is surprising to note that over 71% SMC members did not respond to this extremely important issue.

One of the core empowering provision of the RTE for the disadvantaged groups and weaker section students is the reservation of 25% seats for admissions in the private unaided schools. The government is to reimburse these schools for the same. But the fact is that over 75% headmasters claim that they had not received any reimbursement punctually.

(xv) Ratio of the School's expenses and reimbursement by government for 25% quota admissions

The private unaided school's per child expenditure has been higher than the government schools but they get reimbursement as per government norms, which may be less than the actual expenditure. This is the main reason for the opposition to the 25% reservation admissions by private unaided schools.

This question is relevant to unaided private schools only. Over 9% headmasters noted that the government reimbursement for expenditure per student under 25% quota was below the reimbursement received from the government. Over 18% headmasters and one SMC member said that the reimbursement for this quota was sufficient. This question was not applicable to 72.73% headmaster respondents.

Inadequate or irregular or non-reimbursement of the per capita students expenditure by the government infringes on the most basic provision of access for the disadvantaged groups and weaker section student under the right to education act. If the government, with provision of the RTE act, has forced the unaided private school to fill up 25% of their seats with deprived neighbourhood students it is the duty of the government to reimburse the actual amount of expenditure per student, that varies with the quality each unaided private school displays. Reimbursing these schools with average government per student expenditure is not only unjust to these schools but creates huge obstacles for the neighbourhood socio-economically deprived students to be accommodated socially and educationally in the school atmosphere.

(xvi) School's action, if reimbursement less than expenditure

It has been observed in the other studies and news published in the newspapers that most of the private unaided schools that admitted under the 25% quota as per RTE norms gave discriminatory treatment to the students unable to pay the school fees. The researcher tried to perceive the reality about such issues in surveyed schools and the responses are as follows:

School's action if received reimbursement lower than expenditure

Sr. No.	School's action	Pune		Beed		Total	
		Head-master	SMC Member	Head-master	SMC Member	Head-master	SMC Member
1.	Deficit amount collected from the admitted student	02 (6.06)	00 (00)	00 (00)	00 (00)	02 (6.06)	00 (00)
2.	School did not admit the students unable to pay the fees	00 (00)	00 (00)	02 (6.06)	00 (00)	02 (6.06)	00 (00)
3.	Adjust with received fund	02 (6.06)	00 (00)	02 (6.06)	01 (3.57)	04 (12.12)	01 (3.57)
4.	School did not provide the facilities to students who could not pay the fees	00 (00)	00 (00)	00 (00)	00 (00)	00 (00)	00 (00)
5.	Not applicable	14 (42.42)	06 (21.43)	11 (33.33)	00 (00)	25 (75.76)	06 (21.43)
6.	No Response	00 (00)	08 (28.57)	00 (00)	13 (46.43)	00 (00)	21 (75)
Total		**18 (54.54)**	**14 (50)**	**15 (45.46)**	**14 (50)**	**33 (100)**	**28 (100)**

Contrary to the spirit and the letter of the RTE act two headmasters admitted that they collected the post-reimbursement deficit amount from the students admitted under the 25% quota. While two headmasters from Beed said that they did not admit the student who was unable to pay the deficient fee amount post-reimbursement. While over 12% headmasters said that they had adjusted with the reimbursed amount by the school taking the extra expenditure load of the students admission under the quota. Very high 82.61% SMC members did not give any response to this question.

This data clearly shows that the government is unjust with the expenditure issues of the private unaided school while in turn these schools mated the same injustice to students from the disadvantaged groups and weaker section by denying them admission under this quota. This simply highlights the necessity of the government to reimburse the actual expenditure to private unaided schools so that they create a comfortable atmosphere for the students under this quota. The maladministration of this most important provision for the students from the disadvantaged groups and weaker sections actually warrants a revisit of this provision. The government could withdraw this forceful intervention into private unaided schools and instead focus on raising the overall quality of the public aided schools.

(xvii) Suggestions for better implementation of the 25% reservation by parents and SMC members

Section 12 of the RTE act 2009 has made it compulsory for every private unaided school to admit at least 25% of its entry-level class from the children belonging to economically weaker and disadvantaged groups. Due to some hurdles, the proper implementation of this policy has a question mark. The researcher asked the parents and SMC members their suggestions for better implementation of this policy.

Suggestions for better implementation of 25% Quota

Sr. No.	Response	Pune		Beed		Total	
		Parents	SMC Member	Parents	SMC Member	Parents	SMC Member
1.	Make parents aware about RTE	00 (00)	00 (00)	01 (3.57)	00 (00)	01 (3.57)	00 (00)
2.	Need Proper implementation of 25% reserve seats.	00 (00)	00 (00)	00 (00)	04 (14.29)	00 (00)	04 (14.29)
3.	Need to check the reality of parents like social & economic backwardness	01 (3.57)	02 (7.14)	00 (00)	04 (14.29)	01 (3.57)	06 (21.43)
4.	Not Applicable	13 (46.43)	06 (21.43)	08 (28.57)	00 (00)	21 (75)	06 (21.43)
5.	No Response	01 (3.57)	06 (21.43)	04 (14.29)	06 (21.43)	05 (17.86)	12 (42.85)
	Total	**15 (53.57)**	**14 (50)**	**13 (46.13)**	**14 (50)**	**28 (100)**	**23 (100)**

One parent said that most of the parents did not have proper information about this act. So the government agencies and the schools have to take more efforts to bring about awareness about the right to education act. Over 14.29% SMC members from Beed district want the proper implementation of this act, but they did not give any specific suggestion. That's why one parent and over 21% SMC members said that the schools have to check the parent's real socio-economic status for consideration of admission under this quota since many persons presented bogus certificates to gain the benefits of the policy without being eligible for it. 17.86% parents and 42.85% SMC members did not give any suggestion.

For effective implementation of the 25% reservation quota seats in private schools, there is a need to ensure a fair selection process, an adequate and timely government reimbursement mechanism. We could learn from the Finnish RTE act which is one of the best in the world. The act provides for the local authority to assign to a child of compulsory school age and other receiving education under this act a neighbourhood school. Any procedural obstacles for children and their parents for approaching neighbourhood school for admission in the neighbourhood is school completely avoided in the Finnish system.

5.6 Learning capacity of students from disadvantaged groups and weaker sections

Socio-economic and educational background has implications on the learning capacity of the students. Students from socio-economically poor background may be victims of such circumstances. The researcher asked teachers about the learning capacity of these students and the responses are as follows:

Teacher perception of learning capacity of student's from disadvantaged groups and weaker sections

Sr. No.	Response	Pune	Beed	Total	Percent
1.	Low compared to other students	04	01	05	**13.51**
2.	Equal as other students	03	04	07	**18.92**
3.	Don't know	02	01	03	**8.11**
4.	No Response	13	09	21	**56.76**
Total		**22**	**15**	**37**	**100.00**

Five teacher respondents said that the learning capacity of students from disadvantaged groups and weaker sections is low compared to other students. 18.92% teachers said it was equal to other students, 8.11% displayed ignorance on the issue and 56.76% teachers simply did not respond to this query.

This would mean that a significant number of teachers felt that the students from disadvantaged groups and weaker sections could not cope with the learning process as well as other student. A significant over 8 percent could not respond to this query and a huge over 56% teachers simply did not respond to this query meant that a huge number of teachers neglected keeping track of the academic progress of the students from disadvantaged groups and weaker sections or were simply irresponsible teachers.

Efforts taken to improve the learning capacity of the students from disadvantaged groups and weaker sections:

It is the prime responsibility of the teachers to improve all academic aspects of all the students. Due to weak socio-economic conditions, learning capacity of the students from disadvantaged groups and weaker sections may be lower. Teachers have to take more efforts to improve the learning capacity of the students from disadvantaged groups and weaker sections. The researcher asked about the efforts and the responses are as follows:

Special efforts taken for educational improvement of the students from disadvantaged groups and weaker sections - Teachers

Sr. No.	Response	Pune	Beed	Total	Percent
1.	Yes	12	6	**18**	**48.65**
2.	No	2	3	**5**	**13.51**
3.	No Response	8	6	**14**	**37.84**
Total		**22**	**15**	**37**	**100.00**

As evident from the data, 48.65% teachers gave positive responses saying that they were responsible and took special efforts for the overall improvement of the students from disadvantaged groups and weaker sections. Significant 13.51% teachers did not take any efforts for improvement of these students. Moreover, 37.84% teachers did not give any response and could be construed to have not taken any efforts.

It means that over 48% teachers took special efforts to improve the educational quality of the students from disadvantaged groups and weaker section. However, it is shocking to note that over 13% teachers did not take any special efforts and over 37% teachers simply did not respond to this query showing a tendency of neglect of or prejudice against students from difficult socio-economic background. This is a matter of not just extra training but motivation and social sensitisation for the teachers by government agencies, school management and credible NGO interventions.

Further the researcher asked the teachers about the kinds of efforts taken for educational improvement of the students from the disadvantaged groups and weaker section. The teachers suggested the following activities:

Among teacher respondents, 48.65% have worked for the improvement of the students from the disadvantaged groups and weaker sections. In that, 21.62% reported that they arranged extra remedial classes for these students and only 8.11% said that they distributed learning material to these students. However, 18.92% did not give any response.

It means some teachers arranged for learning facilities for the students from disadvantaged groups and weaker section, but over 18% teachers having said that they took extra efforts could not specify these extra efforts in this query. This exposes some teacher responses and exposes non serious attitude towards learning of the students from deprived communities. Teachers need to be give extra time and teaching aid resources along with socio-economic sensitisation to deal with students from difficult backgrounds.

5.7 Social Distance and Inclusiveness

Social Distance describes the cultural alienation between two groups of the society. India includes different groups based on socio-cultural and economical characteristics. These different groups were socially stratified and maintained social distance among them. This type of tendency is a big obstacle for inclusiveness. The researcher tried to find out the social behaviour of the students from their teacher. The responses are as follows:

Social distance, found, if any, between students from disadvantaged groups and weaker sections and other students-Teacher

Sr. No.	Response	Pune	Beed	Total	Percent
1.	No Response	08	05	13	**18.92**
2.	Yes	01	00	01	**02.70**
3.	No	13	10	23	**62.16**
	Total	**22**	**15**	**37**	**100.00**

As evident from the data most of the teachers (62.16%) replied that there was no social distance among the students. Moreover, 18.92% teachers did not give any response but significantly, one teacher noticed the social distance among the children.

It means most of the students interacted innocently with each other without carrying any prejudices. But one teacher noticed this type of deviant behaviour, which was a significant input. Even when this question regarding social distance between students was a very socially sensitive and delicate question for the teacher still one teacher was courageous to speak out the fact. Further on querying this teacher about his action to reduce this type of behaviour he responded with underlining his efforts to keep unity in the class.

This matter of social relationships being affected due to social distance between students or between the teacher and the pupil is the greatest dissuading factor against learning or education for the students from the socio-economically deprived communities of the society. This is a huge issue and could be addressed only with persistent sensitisation and monitoring the social atmosphere of the classroom by the school management and concerned government agencies. The Srilankan act on right to education provides for teachers' sensitisation on gender issues during the pre-service and in-service training. India being a socially stratified society necessitates sensitisation on social issues during the pre-service and in-service training.

The researcher asked the teachers about the participation of the students from disadvantaged groups and weaker section in sports activities. Students can participate in such activities only in the absence of social distance. Over 40% teachers said that these students participated in the sports activities with the other students. But, still over 8% underlined that these students did not participate in the sports activities. 51.35% teachers did not give any response. This means that the seeds of inequality, even though in a small scale are incidentally or otherwise sown in the school atmosphere. The teacher needs to be sensitised and has to take efforts to eradicate such divisive tendencies from the classroom and the schools. He has to inspire the students for socially inclusive learning and shared relationships.

The 25% reservation quota is for the disadvantaged groups comprising of the scheduled caste and tribe students and the weaker section that is the economically poor students. We have a history of social differentiation with the scheduled castes and tribes so the matter of probing social distance among the SC, ST and other students is significant. Over 62% teachers replied that there was no social distance maintained with the SC, ST students but significantly, one teacher acknowledged that social distance was maintained against the SC, ST students.

The issue of social relationships on caste basis is very delicate and burdened with social pressure, so it is very significant that even then one teacher said that social distance which ultimately meant social discrimination was prevalent against SC, ST students. The issue of social distance/discrimination is one highlighting factor that goes against the assimilative or integrative proposition of SC, ST and poor students coming under the 25% quota with the other relatively affluent students of the private unaided schools. Apart from the 25% quota students not matching up to the over and above necessary expenses of the private unaided schools, the maintenance of social distance/discrimination keeps the SC, ST students individually and communally alienated from the mainstream culture of the private unaided schools. Considering the private unaided schools resentment against filling up the 25% quota seats, the untimely and in-adequate reimbursement of the quota admission from the government and the denial of cultural assimilation of the students by the school systems and the other students warrants a major amendment to the RTE act. And that is of completely withdrawing the provision of 25% quota for the disadvantaged and weaker section students. This conclusion was forced on us due to the huge implementation issues of this quota and the incessant resentment and alienation of the management and affluent students of the private unaided schools against the students from neighbourhood deprived communities.

The issue of social distance can be resolved by a healthy and dynamic relationship between the teacher and the students for a holistic development of knowledge and skills among the students. But as discussed earlier a socially prejudiced mindset carried by a teacher, partially evident from our survey data, makes the SC, ST students, coming under the 25% admission quota, all the more vulnerable to developing an inferiority complex leading to academic decay or ultimate school drop-out/push out.

Public approach is the original approach to education of societies across the world. It stands for carrying over the culture encompassing the traditions and evolving with modernity and its tools of utility. Its aim was and is individual excellence but in the overall framework of public interest. Traditionally in this public approach for education the social studies have been given as much importance as the sciences and maths in pursuit of a balance between individual and technical excellence, but for the overall interest of the framework of social relations and the community at large. Profit motive had limited space. Now especially after the onset of the process of globalisation, liberalisation and privatisation education is fully commodified. Private initiative, pursuit of knowledge inclined towards employability and entrepreneurship is a good idea. This is a need of the contemporary market driven society. This leads to individualism and utilitarianism with greater profit motive and ultimately to competition starting in primary education itself. The simple reasoning being- the more one spends on private education the more one is under pressure to achieve returns, especially financial through profit. The public approach of education has a more holistic approach even when the ultimate motive is of individual excellence and entrepreneurship for financial gains, even if in a subtle manner, molded for overall community prosperity. Democracy and modernity along with globalisation demand commoditisation and privatisation of education for competition and utilitarian excellence but our country is still lagging behind on the socio-economic indicators of poverty, social justice and industrialisation. The state in India still has a lot of work to do as a welfare state so instead of enforcing educational upliftment of the backward and poor classes on private educational initiatives it should delete provisions such as the 25% reservation quota in private un-aided schools and instead make adequate financial allocations for education and raise the overall quality of public schools in India.

This proposition of all round improvement of public school is lately being implemented in the state of Delhi where an attempt is being made to make public schools as good as private schools with adequate financial budget allocations. Essence of attempts to raise quality of all schools of the society can be understood by right to education provisions of other countries such as China. Article 13 of the Chinese RTE act provides for - Peoples government at or above the county level and the administrative department for education shall promote balanced development among schools by narrowing the difference in the conditions for school running and shall not divide the schools in to key and non-key schools. And the schools shall not divide the classes in to key and non-key classes.

This provision underlines the necessity of the state efforts to improve quality of all public schools so should the Indian state put their efforts in raising the overall quality of public schools rather than forcing private schools to share their responsibility and at the same time owing up with the states inability to implement quality school education.

5.8 Discriminatory treatment to the child in school

Every private unaided school has to admit 25% students from the disadvantaged groups and sections in the entry-level class according to the section 12 (1)(c) of this act. It has to ensure that children from the weaker sections should not get discriminatory treatment, segregation from other children in the class room, denial of participation in programmes apart from regular periods.

The researcher asked the parents, students and age appropriate admitted students about discriminatory treatment but all of them gave a negative response. It means no child faced any discriminatory treatment by the school or any personnel of the school.

(i) Seating arrangement of the marginalised children

Happily, the students from the surveyed schools did not report any discriminatory treatment. This is a very positive contemporary aspect in schooling under implementation of the RTE act. But this free and equitable atmosphere is not reflected in the overall outcomes of the students from the disadvantaged and weaker section which is reflected by the demand and acceptance of the deletion of the no-detention policy under the RTE by the government. It is thoroughly documented that detention or drop out have been the highest among the SC, ST and poor students all along the post-independence period.

Seating arrangement of children at school -Parents

Sr. No.	Response	Pune	Beed	Total	Percent
1.	Same as like other students	15	09	24	85.71
2.	Separate from other students	00	00	00	0.00
3.	Don't know	00	00	00	0.00
4.	If any other	00	00	00	0.00
5.	No Response	00	04	04	14.29
	Total	**15**	**13**	**28**	**100**

Another positive observation in the school survey was that none of the parents reported any discrimination in seating arrangement of the students from the marginalised communities. This represents halt of any blatant social discrimination in the teaching-learning dynamics of the classroom. This also is a positive outcome of the objectives of the RTE to achieve social parity for a healthy atmosphere for learning.

(ii) Treatment to children by teacher

The researcher asked the parents about how the teacher behaved with their children in the school and the responses are as follows:

Table - How teachers behave with your child compared to other students- parents

Sr. No.	Response	Pune	Beed	Total	Percent
1.	Neglected	00	00	00	0.00
2.	As usual	15	09	24	85.71
3.	No Response	00	04	04	14.29
	Total	**15**	**13**	**28**	100.00

Here again over 85% parents noted that the teachers behaved with their child as they did with other children. But over 14% parents did not respond to this query. This being a socially sensitive query makes it a matter of concern of why these parents did not respond to this important question.

(iii) Complaints against school regarding discriminatory treatment and other issues

All students from 8th, 9th standards and Age Appropriate Admitted Students (AAAS) reported that, they did not experience discriminatory treatment in the seating arrangement in the teaching process or while playing games, or even during mid day meals and drinking water. None of the parents had registered any complaints with the SMC regarding any discriminative treatment to their wards. Along with this positivity none of the parent has reported about any teacher to have discriminated against students from 8th, 9th and AAAs on the basis of caste, religion or gender.

With all the positivities of the above discussed social non-discrimination paradigms in school we may understand the enacted provision of the Chinese RTE the article 15 of which states – Teacher shall treat students equally in instruction and teaching, and pay attention to the individual differences of students - the teachers need to promote their full development. Proper provision of clause for healthy social relationships in the school between teachers and students and among students themselves need to be expressly made in the RTE.

5.9 Grievance and Redressal

In Pune district 7.14% (2) parents reported that the school denied admissions to the pupil since their parents were uneducated and could not speak in English. But the parents did not register any complaint to any grievance redressal authority since they were simply unaware of this mechanism.

The researcher asked the members of the school management committee about any complaint registered with the SMC regarding 25% admission quota. In response 50% members of SMC not respond to this question, 28.57% member gave negative response there was no complaint registered to the SMC regarding admission of 25% quota.

Grievance redressal mechanism is setup by the government to address and give justice to parents/students in the case of denial of their right to free and compulsory education. The mechanism for this redressal is the government machinery represented by the education department locally right up to the apex institution of the national commission for protection of child rights, in an ascending appellate order.

It is interesting to note that the state grievance redressal mechanism is mandated and expected to give justice for aggrieved parents/students against their own government branch/education department. It is a matter of conjecture whether a state grievance redressal mechanism can dispense justice to parent/students with action against the state's own service provider agencies viz. the education department. Actually, the grievance redressal mechanism should be as autonomous as our independent judiciary to really dispense justice for grievances under the RTE especially to the students from the disadvantaged groups and weaker sections.

The grievance and redressal provision should allow any parent to register a complaint for denial of admission by any school to the local education officer, SMC chairperson or to the state commission for protection of child rights. Three schools from the surveyed districts had denied admissions under the 25% reservation quota but no parents had registered any complaint to any of the concerned authorities. It means the parents were unaware about the avenues of grievance redressal provided under the RTE act.

The grievance and redressal mechanism especially at the local, city or district level where it is manned by the educational authorities need to be revisited. Along with the educational department mechanism, the local credible NGOs working in the field of education should be legally involved to give justice to incidents of grievance regarding admission and other issues under the RTE act. Besides multifaceted publicity of the grievance redressal mechanism with communication connectivity should be created right up to the village level for easy access to justice for all.

5.10 Finance for RTE

The RTE act provides for statutory blinding of provision of funds from the center and the states for implementation of the act. But our survey reveals financial shortages in a number of ways. The field data reveals a number of schools not receiving adequate and timely reimbursement for the admissions of the disadvantaged and weaker section students under the 25% neighbourhood admissions quota.

Further the survey reveals a number of schools that levied various charges as school fees on the students even when the right to education is completely free. No worthwhile social welfare activity is achieved without substantial financial provision for the same. Most developed and even developing countries along with a few underdeveloped countries allocate over 6% of their GDP for education. While in India the same is just 4.05 (2011) of the GDP. More funds are required to enhance quality and quantity of the schools in India. As discussed earlier the RTE focuses more on a continuous and comprehensive evaluation of students than on a comprehensive curriculum for the same. The enhanced learning resources, teacher training, dynamic engagement with the social and economic entities of the neighbourhood of the school based on an interdisciplinary curriculum woven with action and ideas shall need far more resources than allocated at present. Only this approach of holistic learning shall accommodate the strengths of the social diversity of the society and shall lead to social inclusion which is the primary objective of the RTE act.

So to make a success of the implementation of the RTE act the government has to allocate at least 6% of its GDP for education as recommended far back by the Kothari Commission in 1966. For additional resources for education the government may collect and redirect the corporate social responsibility funds of private industries to the education sector and also encourage any private entity to donate for this educational endeavour. To understand the binding provisions for financial allocation we may understand the same provision in the Chinese right to education act as follows:

Provisions for Guarantee of funds-

Article 18. The state places compulsory education completely within the scope of financial guarantee and the funds for compulsory education shall be guaranteed by the state council and the local peoples governments at various levels according to the provisions of this law.

Article 19. The state encourages public organisations and individuals to make donations to compulsory education and encourages the establishment of foundations for compulsory education in accordance with the state regulations governing the administration of foundations.

The percentage of increase in government funds allotted for compulsory education by the state council and the local peoples governments of various levels shall be higher than the percentage of increase in regular government revenues in order to ensure the gradual increase in the average amount of funds for compulsory education per student in school, in the salaries of the teaching staff and in the average amount of funds per student for public use.

5.1 Continuous and Comprehensive Evaluation (CCE)

(i) What is CCE

Continuous and comprehensive evaluation is the process of assessment mandated by the RTE Act 2009. In this new evaluation system the student's marks have been replaced with grades which have been decided through the continuous (whole year) curricular and extra-curricular evaluations. These are efforts to decrease the pressure on the students faced while learning and giving small test and examination along with extra-curricular activities throughout the academic year. The grades are awarded to the students based on the learning abilities as well as skills, innovation, teamwork, speaking and behavioural changes etc. The measures for the evaluation of the student's abilities through CCE are formulated by the relevant state governments as well as by the Central Board of Secondary Education in India.

The persons who have direct or indirect concern with school education system like Headmaster, Teacher and parents also need to be well versed about such an evaluation system. The researcher asked all the three on this issue and the responses are as follows:

As indicated in the data 60 percent Headmasters from the both districts and 13.63% Teachers and 13.33% parents from Pune district said CCE is a very good evaluation method, it covers all aspect of the child's behaviour it needs proper implementation. 9.09% Teachers from Pune and 20% from Beed district accepted goodness of the CCE but felt the teacher have to do lot of clerical work regarding the CCE assessment. The teachers have to expend their valuable time on the regular preparation and maintenance of the records than spending time on teaching.

22.45% of the respondents from the both districts mentioned that this is a school-based assessment of students, which covered all aspects of student's development process. They thought that the students could do a lot of activities without mental pressure and the teacher could pay individual attention. 18.18% teachers and one parent from Pune and 40% teachers and 15.38% parents from Beed district said that it was the behavioural observation of the students.

27.79% Headmasters from Pune and 13.33% from Beed district said that it was a not good evaluation method instead the annual examination system was better than CCE. 9.09% teachers from Pune along with one headmaster and 20% teachers along with 7.69% parents from Beed district did not know about the CCE. More than 60% parents from both districts have no information about CCE but gave irrelevant answer.

The CCE invited a mixture of positive and negative responses. It is a crucial component of the RTE but is unfulfilled without a complimenting comprehensive curriculum. Even though most of the respondents said the CCE is good but the researcher noted the negative approach about the CCE. There is a need of expert training to all the persons who has direct concern with school education, especially the Headmasters and teachers.

(ii) Tools used for the CCE

Continuous and comprehensive evaluation is a process of assessment by the teacher throughout the academic year. The level of knowledge and participation in practical, team activities and extracurricular activities are the objects of assessment for the all-round improvement of the students. Teachers are engaged in the teaching-learning process and give cumulative and comprehensive judgment about a students' progress. The assessment involves tests (written, oral), assignments, projects, fieldwork, discussion, practical work, class-work etc.

The researcher asked the headmaster, teacher and students from the 8th and 9^{th}standard about the tools used for assessing the student's academic and behavioural progress and the responses are as follows:

Almost all of the respondents including headmasters, teachers, 8th and 9th standard students from Pune and Beed said that a number of tools were used under the CCE for assessing the behavioral changes in the students i.e. daily observation, oral exam, various activities, practical, homework, test exam and written exam.

Only over 4% 8th standard students from Pune and over 3% 8th standards students from Beed said that except project work all the above mentioned tools were used for evaluation. Over 10% 9th standard students from Pune and 15% 9th standards students from Beed said that observation, oral exam, activities and practicals were the tools for comprehensive evaluation. Over 3% 8th standard students from Pune and over 2% students from Beed said that practical, test and homework were the tools used for the continuous and comprehensive evaluation. And over 4% teachers from Pune used daily observation as the tool for continuous and comprehensive evaluation.

(iii) Daily observation of the student's behaviour and CCE

Education is concerned with the all round development (physical, emotional and intellectual) of the children. All aspects of the personality development of students have to be assessed by the teacher. Continuous and comprehensive evaluation covers all scholastic and co-curricular areas of the school education. This evaluation includes two types of assessment, summative and formative. Formative assessment covers academic areas and summative covers non-academic areas like attitudes and skills. This has to be evaluated by observation in the class and outside activities. For the formative assessment teachers have to observe continuously all aspects of the student's behaviour and record it in the observation book. The researcher asked the teachers about this type of assessment and the responses are as follows:

It is revealed from the above table that most of the teachers (91.89%) note down the observational aspects in the observational book. Only one gave a negative response and 5.41% did not give any response.

It means that most of the teachers note the proper observational entries on the observation books or register. The researcher asked about the nature of observation and the responses are as follows:

The data shows the nature of the observation of academic and co-curricular activities. Most of the teachers (35.14%) reported that they assess the students for his/her regularity and his/her participation in games and various activities. Moreover, 24.32% respondents said that they check the individual skills of the students. 29.73%

respondents keep the record at the time of teaching on observation of the students' learning. Only 5.41% teachers assess the student by asking questions and only two teachers from Pune district did not give any response.

It means all the respondents used various techniques to assess the student's co-curricular activities. Along with this the researcher asked the teacher the time of record maintenance of the students' co-curricular activities and the responses are as follows:

Learning is a continuous process so the teacher has to assess the student's learning capabilities continuously. The teacher has to take observational notes continuously. Among the teachers 47.95% teachers reported that they enlisted the complete emotional and intellectual changes of the students at the time of teaching. Also 13.51% teachers said that they registered the changes at any time, similarly the same number of teachers told that they registered all changes at the end of the week, 5.44% said they took it in a month and 13.51% did not give any response.

It means most of the teachers enlisted all positive and negative changes deriving in the student's attitude while learning in the class or outside it. This is the correct way to assess the student's attitude/ skills or other aspects of the personality. Nevertheless, the researcher noted that some teachers did not enlist it in the classroom or listed it after a long period. In such type of assessment, the observations might be prejudiced and which may affect the improvement of the students.

(iv) Activities done for effective CCE

Education is the process of personality development. CCE is the process of the overall personality development of the child. Teachers have to evaluate the students accurately on their behavioural changes. He/she has to know the whole process, tools of evaluation and methods of evaluation. The effectiveness of the CCE mostly depends on the activeness of the teacher. The researcher asked all teachers about the activities done by him/her and by the school for effective evaluation.

As indicated in the above data of the headmasters and teachers (80%) said that the school sent the teachers for training on CCE. One teacher and 33.33% headmasters from Pune and one headmaster from Beed said generally the school called meetings to give instruction to the teachers or sent them for proper training or arranged informative lectures for teacher on evaluation by CCE. 44.44% Headmaster from Pune and 93.33% from Beed district said they keep watch on the evaluation process for accurate evaluation along with other activities done for effective CCE. Three (13.64%) teachers from Pune and one from Beed said that they did not take any extra efforts for the effective evaluation of the students through CCE.

It means that most of the teachers are trained for the CCE and some time the headmasters keep watch on the evaluation process.

(v) Perception of possibility of accurate evaluation by CCE

The researcher found a lot of misunderstanding in the school related to continuous and comprehensive evaluation. Most of the headmasters and teachers were unhappy with this evaluation method. Most of the respondents replied that with the CCE we couldn't evaluate the students properly and the annual exam was the best way for correct evaluation of the students. Here the researcher asked the headmasters and teachers about the possibility of accurate evaluation by CCE and the responses are as follows –

Table - Perception of possibility of accurate evaluation by CCE

Sr. No.	Response	Pune		Beed		Total	
		Head-master	Teacher	Head-master	Teacher	Head-master	Teacher
1.	Yes	09 (50)	14 (63.63)	11 (73.34)	11 (73.34)	20 (60.61)	25 (67.57)
2.	No	02 (11.11)	06 (27.27)	02 (13.33)	03 (20)	04 (12.12)	09 (24.32)
3.	Yes, little bit	07 (38.89)	01 (4.55)	02 (13.33)	00 (00)	09 (27.27)	01 (2.70)
4.	Can't say	00 (00)	00 (00)	00 (00)	00 (00)	00 (00)	00 (00)
5.	Don't know	00 (00)	01 (4.55)	00 (00)	01 (6.66)	00 (00)	02 (5.41)
Total		**18 (100)**	**22 (100)**	**15 (100)**	**15 (100)**	**33 (100)**	**37 (100)**

As indicated in the data 60.61% headmaster and 67.57% teachers said accurate evaluation of the students is possible by CCE. 27.27% headmasters and 2.70% teachers said only a little bit accuracy has been possible in the evaluation by CCE. 12.12% headmasters and 24.32% teachers from the both districts gave a negative response.

It means most of the respondents gave positive response about the possibility of accurate evaluation by CCE.

(vi) Merits and Demerits of the CCE

CCE is a holistic assessment system aiming to evaluate skills of students in all areas in order to create an atmosphere for joyful learning. Moreover, education is the process of personality development and it is a continuous process that needs to be assessed for continued evaluation. CCE is good for evaluation of the all-round personality development of the child but it has many drawbacks also. Many teachers have not fully understood the strength of the CCE and so a lot of them oppose it.

The researcher asked all teachers to explain the merits and demerits of the CCE and the responses are as follows:

Table - Explain the merits and demerits of the CCE - Teachers

Sr. No.	Response	Pune	Beed	Total
1.	Evaluation of various activities is not good and Marks system is better than grade	06 (27.27)	05 (33.33)	11 (29.73)
2.	This is good system but it runs for too long	03 (13.64)	03 (20)	06 (16.22)
3.	It is good for all round development of students and students of weaker section, but Students didn't work seriously so they will faced difficulties in 9th	07 (31.82)	02 (13.33)	09 (24.32)
4.	Need for changes in summative evaluation; Evaluation of various activities is good method.	02 (9.09)	00 (00)	02 (5.41)
5.	Students from disadvantaged groups and weaker sections can't complete the projects due to their weak economic condition	00 (00)	01 (6.67)	01 (2.70)
6.	All aspects of personality can be evaluated by CCE, slow learner children were encouraged by this evaluation but it causes loss to clever students, CCE should be fixed up to 5th std.	01 (4.54)	00 (00)	01 (2.70)
7.	It is best policy, No need of change	01 (4.54)	00 (00)	01 (2.70)
8.	No Response	02 (9.09)	04 (26.67)	06 (16.22)
	Total	**22 (100)**	**15 (100)**	**37 (100)**

The researcher got both negative and positive responses for this question. Near about 30% teachers did not like this evaluation system in that the teacher respondents, 27.27% out of 22 from Pune and 33.33% out of 15 respondents from Beed district, said evaluation by various activities is not good and the marks system is better than grade system. 30% teachers said that correct evaluation cannot be possible by CCE. Moreover, 16.22% teachers said in the annual examination the teacher can evaluate the students by their performance in the paper but the CCE takes long time to evaluate. One teacher said that this policy is not affordable for economically poor students because the students from such category cannot prepare the projects assigned by the school.

There are many positive responses also given by the teacher. Among all teacher respondents 13.64% from Pune and 20% from Beed said that CCE is good for all round development of students and students of the disadvantaged groups and weaker sections, but students didn't work seriously so they faced difficulties in 9th standard. Two (9.09%) teachers from Pune district said evaluation by various activities is good, but there was no need to organise written exam like tests in the class, so there was need for change in summative evaluation. One teacher from Pune said that this policy is helpful to slow learners but it is not good for clever students, it should be fixed up to 5th standard only. One teacher from Pune said this is a good policy and there is no need for any change in this policy.

It means that a lot of teachers have negative approach about the CCE but they need proper guidance on the CCE.

(vii) Efforts taken for the educational improvement of the students

It is the primary responsibility of the school to develop all the aspects of the student's personality. As per RTE Act, no student is retained in the same class till 8th standard. Teachers have to take responsibility of the educational improvement of the students who lag behind in the CCE or get D grade in the evaluation. They can arrange extra classes or re-test for these students. The researcher asked the teachers about their efforts and the responses are as follows:

As stated by the teachers nearly 60% of the teachers said that they arranged the extra remedial classes to improve the acquired grades of the students. 22.73% teachers from Pune said their school re-organize the test or other activities for the students who could not attend the test or other activities arranged by the school.

However, 03(13.63%) teachers from Pune and 05 (26.66%) from Beed district said no students were available in the class from such category and one from Pune said he had not taken extra efforts for the improvement of the students. One teacher from Beed district did not give any response to this question.

It means that nearly all teachers took educational improvement of the students as their prior responsibility.

(viii) Teaching Aids used by teachers

Teaching Aids are necessary now a days for effective teaching. Teaching aids are helpful in attracting the attention of the students in the classroom. It makes learning permanent because learning with the use of more than one sense of the five senses of touch, sight, hearing, smelling and feeling is more effective for a prolonged period. There are many audio-visual tools usually used for teaching by the teachers. i.e. picture, maps, charts, radio, T.V., recorder, projector, slides etc. The researcher asked the teacher about the teaching aids that they used while teaching and the responses are as follows:

As a response 59.09% of the teachers from Pune and 93.33% from Beed district replied they used the teaching aids as per requirement of the topic. 31.82% teachers from Pune district said that they used graphs, globe, board and picture as well as audio tools for teaching. One from Beed did not respond to this question.

It means that most of the teachers are using teaching aids in their classroom teaching. It is good for the students because it makes the learning process simpler.

(ix) Teaching Method

Teaching method is also an important part of the learning process. Learning of the students generally depends on the teaching of the teacher. A good teacher generally uses a teaching method as per topic or the acquiring capacity of the students. The teaching method used as per requirement may make the learning process easy. There are lots of teaching methods available i.e. lecturing, demonstrating, classroom discussion etc. Generally, at the school level teachers need to teach with simpler methods which makes learning joyful. The researcher asked the teachers about their teaching methods and the responses are as follows:

Data shows that most of the teachers used more than one teaching method for effective teaching. In all 50% teachers from Pune and 66.66% from Beed district said they used lecturing, classroom discussion, question-answering and experimental teaching methods while teaching in the classroom. Only one teacher from Pune said he used only exploratory teaching method. 13.64% teachers from Pune said they used only lecturing, discussion and question-answering method. One from Pune district said he used all the methods including drama. One from Beed did not give any response.

It means most of the teachers used more than one teaching method for effective teaching. They used a method as per requirement of the subject and topic. It is good for healthy classroom interactions and joyful learning.

The CCE is a very significant provision of the RTE as it evaluates the academic, physical as well as emotional aspects of the students for a holistic learning. But for a more effective implementation of the CCE the government, the school system and relevant NGOs with credibility, need to put in far more resources and training especially for the teacher who is the core coordinator of the process of CCE. Far more and varied learning aids and ideas for individual and team learning need to be developed and provided. The teacher needs to undergo rigorous and continuous in-service training so as to be able to understand and provide a learning which covers the intellectual, emotional and physical aspects of the students. Moreover, CCE is just an evaluative process. The RTE seems to have, if not totally overlooked, at least given far less attention to a comprehensive curriculum. Because only a comprehensive curriculum would demand a continuous and comprehensive evaluation. The CCE is only a structure without the substance for want of a comprehensive curriculum. A comprehensive curriculum would need to comprise of varied pedagogies, interdisciplinary curriculum, intellectual as well as manual-skills learning with dignity of labour and an inclusive social atmosphere for a holistic learning. The different subjects of social studies, sciences, maths and languages need to be taught in an interwoven manner for awakening a holistic thought process in the young minds of the students. So the RTE needs to accommodate such comprehensive curriculum to compliment an effective evaluative process.

For better understanding and implementation of the RTE we could also learn from similar experienced attempts of neighbouring countries such as Sri Lanka and China.

We need to consider how a comprehensive curriculum could be formulated from the way it is done under *Article 17 of the Chinese free and compulsory education act*- Instruction and teaching shall be carried out in conformity with the pattern of education and the characteristics of students to the need of all students, be oriented to the need of all students and designed to impart knowledge to them by organically integrating moral, intellectual, physical and aesthetic education in instruction and teaching, with special attention paid to developing their of independent thinking, creativity and practice in order to enable them to develop in all round way.

In the last few years our educational policies are moving towards bifurcation general education and vocational education. Students are given the option of going for vocational education at the end of elementary education. This goes against the grain of interdisciplinary education and also of the opportunity to go for higher education. We have discussed learning to be a dynamics of mental and manual skills giving equality of status and incentive to the combined efforts. This is knowledge building with social inclusion because the mental and manual skills of the socially diverse communities of the society are considered for this process.

In this aspect we could learn from our neighbour Sri Lanka which considered knowledge building to be a holistic process. They have made provisions for an interdisciplinary and holistic knowledge building with vocational and life skills provisions in their RTE act itself. The Indian RTE act needs to emulate this.

Article 4 of the Srilankan RTE act-Attempt were made to stream children at the end of primary and basic education stage to academic, technical and vocational steams. However, these proposals were not acceptable to a public who had seen in the past that academic success had led to social mobility. Now efforts are been made to provide a practical element to general education through the development of competencies.

Article 5. An inquiring mind ability for analysis and reasoning the application of knowledge to practical problems and a problem solving approach, knowledge and interest in contemporary social and economic developments in the country. Capacity for leadership and team work, a work ethos with values of productivity and discipline imparted through appropriate learning experiences in suitable technical, vocational subject and most important good communication skills, both oral as well as written, even in the mother tongue, not to mention English.

Article 6. Learning Process-Such a transformation can be brought about by changing the methodology of teaching and learning rather than through the content of education. Of course that does not discount the importance of science and technology in the modern contest. But use of activity based learning techniques such as project work, assignments, discovery methods etc. will sharpen the general skills of students.

Article 7. Flexible learning opportunities and life skills development-The junior secondary state curriculum has introduced life competencies as a subject and practical work and work on small project as an important element. Activity rooms were proposed to be established in schools to enable students to learn by doing thing by themselves, using simple tools and learning simple techniques. In the curriculum for secondary senior stage of GCE O/L technical subject to help student continue learning of life skills, practical work has been made compulsory in the GCE A/L curriculum. It was proposed by the 1998 reform that links be developed between the school system and the vocational and technical training system to provide flexible learning opportunities to student. Career guidance and counseling has been introduced at this stage in order to provide advice to students to enable them to select avenues most suited to their capabilities. Community learning centers have been established under non-formal sector to provide flexible learning opportunities and life skills development to children not being able to attend school.

The current practical technical skills subject area in grades 6 to 9 will be restructured and renamed as technical skills which cover the areas namely, Graphic Arts, Computer Literacy (IT), elementary technology, agriculture, and food preparation

5.12 No Detention Policy

No detention policy is the most important provision in this. The provision invites many positive and negative responses from the society. Many of the stakeholders have not understood the real meaning and objectives of this policy. Section 16 the RTE act provides for no detention policy - 'No child admitted in a school shall be held back in any class or expelled from school till the completion of elementary education.' Along with this section 30(1) stated that no child shall be required to pass any board examination till the completion of elementary education. Many headmasters and teachers as well as parents also define it conveniently. Teachers felt that there was no need to teach and evaluate the students and the students and parents felt there was no need to study.

The researcher found out a lot of misunderstanding regarding this policy. He asked the headmasters and the teachers about no-detention policy and the opinion of both is given below.

Table - Opinion on No Detention Policy

Sr. No.	Responses	Pune		Beed		Total	
		Head-master	Teacher	Head-master	Teacher	Head-master	Teacher
1.	This is a good policy. Students should not be held back. Need proper implementation, teacher also responsible for the failure of the students. He/she had to take more efforts on those students.	04 (12.12)	01 (2.70)	02 (6.06)	00 (00)	06 (18.18)	01 (2.70)
2.	Students get the opportunity of education. No students can be held back or expelled from school, irrespective of academic performance till class 8th.	00 (00)	02 (5.41)	00 (00)	03 (8.11)	00 (00)	05 (13.52)
3.	Student should be hold in same class if it is necessary; It would be helpful to make quality improvement of the students.	14 (42.42)	15 (40.54)	09 (27.27)	00 (00)	23 (69.70)	15 (40.54)
4.	Due to this policy students do not study properly and they could fail in 9th std.	00 (00)	04 (21.62)	03 (9.09)	08 (21.62)	03 (9.09)	12 (32.44)
5.	Could not respond properly	00 (00)	00 (00)	00 (00)	03 (8.10)	00 (00)	03 (8.10)

	No Response	00 (00)	00 (00)	01 (3.03)	01 (2.70)	01 (3.03)	01 (2.70)
	Total	**18 (54.54)**	**22 (59.46)**	**15 (45.46)**	**15 (40.54)**	**33 (100)**	**37 (100)**

The data shows the opinion of the headmasters and teachers on the no-detention policy. Interestingly nearly 70% headmasters and over 40% teachers said that a student should be held back in the same class if necessary to improve his/her quality. While just over 18% headmasters and a miniscule over 3% teacher said that the policy of non-detention was good and that the teacher was also responsible for the failure of the students and required to take extra efforts. Over 13% teachers said that no student should be held back irrespective of academic performance till 8th standard. And over 9% headmasters and over 32% teachers felt that due to this policy the students did not study properly so they could fail in the 9th standard. And over 8% teachers significantly could not respond properly to this query of a most important provision of the RTE.

No Detention policy – Effects on the learning of the student

The researcher realised that there were many negative responses regarding no-detention policy. Most of the stakeholders took convenient meaning or understanding of this crucial policy provision. The researcher asked the teachers and parents about the positive-negative consequences of the no-detention policy on the students' educational progress.

Table - No Detention policy – Effects on the learning of the student

Sr. No.	Response	Pune		Beed		Total	
		Teacher	Parents	Teacher	Parents	Teacher	Parents
1.	Students become careless about studying resulting in stoppage of educational development	01 (2.70)	02 (7.14)	01 (2.70)	04 (14.29)	02 (5.41)	06 (21.43)
2.	Students concentrate more on other activities	00 (00)	02 (7.14)	01 (2.70)	01 (3.57)	01 (2.70)	03 (10.71)
3.	Need to conduct traditional exam as comprehensive evaluation will notevaluate correctly	08 (21.62)	04 (14.29)	00 (00)	04 (14.29)	08 (21.62)	08 (28.58)

4.	All the above	11 (29.73)	07 (25)	12 (32.43)	02 (7.14)	23 (62.16)	09 (32.14)
5.	Learning process become easy because students have no fear of failure	02 (5.41)	00 (00)	00 (00)	00 (00)	02 (5.41)	00 (00)
6.	No response	00 (00)	00 (00)	01 (2.70)	02 (7.14)	01 (2.70)	02 (7.14)
	Total	**22 (59.46)**	**15 (53.57)**	**15 (40.54)**	**13 (46.43)**	**37 (100)**	**28 (100)**

Over 21% parents and over 5% teachers thought that the no-detention policy made students careless about studying resulting in stoppage of educational development. While over 10% parents and 3% teachers felt the students were concentrating on all activities other than studying due to this policy. Significantly over 28% parents and over 21% teachers wanted to have the traditional examination system back as they thought students could not be evaluated properly under the CCE policy. And above 62% teachers and over 32% parents concurred with all the above three implications of the no-detention policy. Only over 5% teachers thought that the learning process became easier for the students due to no fear of failure.

Significantly a majority of teacher and significant number of parents feel that the learning process is affected due to the no-detention policy. This raises question marks on the substance and structure of the learning process under the RTE. This underlines that the no-detention policy has removed fear from the process of learning but the learning process without a comprehensive and relevant curriculum has failed to enthuse joy in the learning process.

It is astonishing that a huge majority of headmasters and significant number of teachers wanted to get back the provision of detaining students. This is the biggest contravention of the most important provision i.e. no-detention policy of the RTE act. As discussed earlier where it was mentioned that the CCE was incomplete without a comprehensive curriculum, similarly the no-detention policy is incomplete without corroborative inputs of teacher-training, multiple pedagogies, interdisciplinary and relevant curriculum, comprehensive evaluation and adequate resources for learning aids and practicals along with dynamic interaction of the school with socio-cultural, commercial and industrial entities of the school neighbourhood. It needs to be underlined that schools are for learning purpose and not for screening out students. It is a well documented fact that school dropouts and class repeating students mostly comprise of the scheduled tribes, the scheduled castes, the DTNTs and the girl child. The yester years policy of detention has been a nemesis to these students who come from underprivileged backgrounds.

The no-detention policy is a major booster for the universalisation of elementary education but here our data exposes that a majority of headmasters and significant number of teachers want the recall of the detention policy. This is a major question mark on the very spirit of opening doors of primary education to all including the SC, ST and others. This is a huge implementation challenge and makes one wonder whether the no-detention policy should be withdrawn for seven years so that the school system and the establishment improves to a level where the question of detention would be irrelevant. This would happen only if radical changes are made as discussed earlier. But the question mark on the withdrawal on this crucial provision shall be discussed in details later.

Traditionally in India from the ancient times scriptural directives prohibited the backward castes from receiving any education, religious or utilitarian. With global cultural exposure during the British and modern times and the onset of democracy underlined by the fundamental rights of liberty, equality and justice giving the right to education to all the communities of the country we have a formal education system for the same. Our education system is based on an examination system leading to individualised competition and screening out of individuals not making it to the required mark. As discussed earlier the social, economic and educational background of the SC and ST students have made them major victims along with some others to be failures and drop outs of the schooling system. The right to education, changing this scenario has brought in the provision of no-detention till the 8th standard for all children. Our data reveals that most of the headmaster and teachers along with some parents oppose the no-detention policy. They contend that due to this policy the teachers are not under the pressure to deliver and the students along with their parents, become negligent of studies with the knowledge of each child being promoted up to 8th standard with or without the prescribed levels of learning. The government has come up with this provision without the substantial backup for its satisfactory implementation. No detention policy actually means ensuring all children received the prescribed levels of learning in each class which would require a thorough overhaul of teacher training, pedagogy curriculum and teaching aids. The teacher needs to be given greater social status, as received in ancient times, far better financial incentive (better than senior college teachers as done in some western countries) and comprehensive and continuous in service training with greater autonomy and responsibility. The curriculum needs to be relevant especially to the school and regional socio-economic domain. It needs to be interdisciplinary interweaving the sciences and the basics of social sciences along with primary activities like agriculture and vocational skills of the region to make it accommodative of the social diversity of the region. Relevance leads to interest that leads to understanding and to ultimate knowledge out puts. Our primary basis of memorisation and presentation for learning has to be complimented by practical activities by a dynamics between the mental skills and manual efficacies. This whole process will make detention irrelevant and obsolete. But given the rate of change of our educational process this radical change is too big a task for the Indian educational system. So the via media could be that the detention policy should be brought back at the 6th standard level. This step is already in the pipeline on the advice of the Central Advisory Board of Education (CABE). This prescription would look socially regressive as it undermines the socio-economic and educational handicaps of the backward caste students but the fact today that large number of students fail in 9th standard because of being promoted up to 8th standard without the prescribed level of learning cannot be overlooked. This simply is due to incompetence of the school system to ensure no-detention along with prescribed levels of learning. The failures of the 9th standard level among others obviously include large numbers of SC and ST students. So in the giving situation it is better to go back to the detention policy so that all stake holders of the school system shall again take troubles and responsibilities of learning. But this can only be a temporary step back for say a period of seven years. No detention is the ideal when all the above prescriptions are implemented to make learning a relevant and joyful process making detention completely irrelevant.

5.13. Age appropriate Admitted students (AAAS)

The right to education act, 2009 provides the right of education to all the children in the age group of 6 to 14 years so that no child remains without education. It is primary responsibility of a school to find out the out of school children within the school neighbourhood and admit them in the appropriate class as per their age. School should provide them with special training of a minimum of three months that could be extendable up to two years.There should be periodic assessment of the learning progress made by such children in the special training on continuous basis. The entry-level assessment will determine the duration of special training in each case and placement in age appropriate class thereafter. The head teacher/teacher must ensure that a consolidated record of all children is maintained in the training centers for better traceability of learning outcomes for necessary interventions.

The school shall maintain a performance record of the children, clearly indicating the progress made during the period of special training at regular intervals, stating the milestones accomplished for further action with regard to children's admission in age appropriate classes. The researcher tried to observe the actual situation of the age appropriate students in the surveyed schools.

(i) Number of age appropriate students admitted in the surveyed school

The researcher asked the headmasters about admission of the age appropriate students in current academic year. Over 94% headmasters from Pune district said that no child was admitted in their schools under the AAAS category. While it was 80% in the case of Beed district. One headmaster from Pune had admitted 24 students under this category while three headmasters from Beed had admitted 8 students in the current academic year.

Pune district survey shows that only one school admitted out of school children and three schools in Beed did the same. The most important objective of the RTE act is universalisation of elementary education and bringing out of school children inside the schooling system is the biggest challenge to this act. Even after the over six years of implementation of the act we still have children out of school proven by our survey data and also documented by the UNESCO report which states that as on 2015, 1.4 million children are out of school in India and 57.8 million globally.[1] These facts raise issues about the sincerity and efficacy of the neighbourhood surveys carried out by school teachers to spot out of school children. These children incidentally come from socially and economically backward classes raising questions about the inclusive efficacy of the RTE act.

(ii) Number of AAAS respondents from both districts

In this study the researcher tried to find out the current situation of age appropriate admitted students. In this study the researcher visited 33 schools from both districts, including government, private aided and unaided schools. Our aim was to interact with minimum two age appropriate admitted students from each school, but we found in all only eleven AAA students in the total number of surveyed school. Out of them 6 (54.55%) were from Pune and 5 (45.45%) were from Beed district. Gender based proportion of the AAA students composed of 45% girls and 54% boys. This suggests that AAA students are nearly equal on the gender ratio.

(iii) Age and class level-wise number of AAAS

Age and class-wise distribution of these students is given in the table below. To get competent responses the researcher tried to interact with students studying in higher classes but on not finding any had to interact with students admitted in lower classes.

Table - Age and class level of the AAA students

Sr. No.	Class	Age in years							Total
		07	10	11	12	13	14	16	
1.	02	01 (9.09)	01 (9.09)	00 (00)	00 (00)	00 (00)	00 (00)	00 (00)	**02 (18.18)**
2.	04	00 (00)	01 (9.09)	00 (00)	00 (00)	00 (00)	00 (00)	00 (00)	**01 (9.09)**
3.	05	00 (00)	01 (9.09)	01 (9.09)	01 (9.09)	01 (9.09)	01 (9.09)	00 (00)	**05 (45.46)**
4.	06	00 (00)	00 (00)	00 (00)	01 (9.09)	00 (00)	00 (00)	00 (00)	**01 (9.09)**
5.	07	00 (00)	00 (00)	00 (00)	00 (00)	00 (00)	01 (9.09)	00 (00)	**01 (9.09)**
6.	09	00 (00)	00 (00)	00 (00)	00 (00)	00 (00)	00 (00)	01 (9.09)	**01 (9.09)**
Total		**01 (9.09)**	**03 (27.28)**	**01 (9.09)**	**02 (18.18)**	**01 (9.09)**	**02 (18.18)**	**01 (9.09)**	**11 (100)**

The researcher found five AAA students in the 5th standard 2 in the 2nd standard and one each in the 4th, 6th, 7th and 8th standards. As seen in the above table we realise that some AAA students have not been admitted in the age appropriate classes. One student aged 10 is seen in the second standard. This 10 year student should have been admitted at least in the 4th or 5th standard. While another couple of students aged 13 and 14 are admitted in the 5th standard. These should have been admitted in the 7th or 8th standard respectively. This mismatch defeats the very purpose of age appropriate admissions which is to make students feel comfortable and belonged to their peer groups. This mismatch exposes the infringement of the AAAS clause of the RTE. But it may also reveal the incompetence of the teaching staff in effectively fast-forwarding the learning process of the AAA students.

(iv) Caste of the AAAS

It has been proved by a number of studies that the majority of the children in out of school admitted category, belong to the socio-economically backward communities. With weak economic conditions, most of the students are migratory or have to contribute in the family earnings and so the drop-out rates are unusually high in these communities. The caste-wise number of AAAS from both the districts is as follows:

Table – Caste-wise Students

Sr. No.	Caste	Total	Percent
1.	Padmashali	01	9.09
2.	Mahar	01	9.09
3.	Banjara	01	9.09
4.	Wadar	02	18.18
5.	Muslim backward class	03	27.27
6.	No Response	03	27.27
Total		**11**	**100**

The data proves that all the surveyed AAA students belong to backward communities proving that the RTE implementation has to reach out to the students from disadvantaged groups, if it has to prove social inclusion as its primary objective.

(v) Person who helped to AAA students to get the admission

It is an important responsibility of the headmaster, teacher, school management committee member / chairperson and local social worker, member of self-governing body to find out the out of school children from the school neighbourhood and admit them in the age appropriate classes. The persons who helped in this process is given below.

As evident from the table above it is clear that 54.55% teachers helped the AAA students get admission while only 9% of headmasters did the same. Moreover, a similar over 18% students said that members of the school management committee and local social workers helped them get admission in the AAA classes. This shows that all students had to take somebody's help to get admission and all relevant persons have actively extended help to these students for admission.

(vi) AAAS - Reasons for late admissions

The researcher tried to find out the reasons for delayed admissions of the AAA students and responses are as follows:

As evident from the table above we can see the reasons for the delay in admission of the age appropriate students. Over 45% respondent alluded their delayed school admissions to their weak economic condition. And over 27% to careless neglect of parents. Over 18% students delayed school admission due to medical ailments and 9% to change in medium of education after primary schooling. All these reasons for delay in school admission imply weak financial conditions, illiteracy and health problems of the families of the AAA students. They represents reasons for the exclusions of the underprivileged community students delayed and stuttering educational progress.

(vii) Training for AAAS

When a AAA student is admitted in to a school he/she has the right to be admitted in to the age appropriate class and have a right to receive special training up to three months and expandable up to two years for fast forward learning of the child to the age appropriate class adjustment of the child in appropriate class. The researcher tried to know the status of special training for the age appropriate students and the responses are as follows:

Table - AAAS training received after admission

Sr. No.	Duration	Pune	Beed	Total	Percent
1.	2 months	02	01	03	**27.27**
2.	3 months	03	00	03	**27.27**
3.	6 months	00	02	02	**18.18**
4.	1 year	01	00	01	**9.10**
5.	Nothing	00	02	02	**18.18**
	Total	**06**	**05**	**11**	**100.00**

The data indicates the percentage of children who got special training as AAA students. A similar over 27% AAA students said that they received 2 months and 3 months special training respectively. Over 18% students received special training for 6 months and only one student received such training for 1 year. 18.18% reported they did not get any kind of training after admission. The later 18% AAA students who did not receive any kind of training is a clear infringement of the rights of out of school children under the RTE act. This discrepancy is a direct obstacle to the inclusive objective of retention and promotion of primary education of the students from underprivileged communities.

(viii) Educational facilities for the AAAS

As per sec 29, (I) of the RTE act the special training for the AAAS shall be based on specially designed, age appropriate learning material, approved by the Academic Authority maybe referred as Special Learning Support Materials (SLSM). The special learning study material has been developed in such manner which enables learners to develop their knowledge and competency levels as per their age, by adopting a condensed curriculum. This will help the learners to bridge the learning gaps to be at par with their peers in short duration. In Maharashtra SCERT, Pune developed the study material for the AAA students. Along with this the schools should take the special efforts for the educational development of these students.

The researcher asked the headmasters, teachers and member of SMC about the availability of such material in their school. Only 33.33% schools have this type of study material for AAA students. In all, 13.51% teachers and 26.09% members of SMC said they got the study material from SCERT, Pune. From this two teachers said they got only books and two said they got books, teacher handbook, evaluation sheets and cards for learning. Moreover, 54.55% Headmasters, 86.49% teachers and 47.83% members of SMC gave negative response and said they did not get any material from anywhere. However, 12.12% headmasters from Pune district said there are no AAA students admitted to their school so they did not seek any SLSM for AAA students.

Only over 33% schools from the number that required SLSM have received study material for AAAS. All teachers have not received the complete sets of SLSM. This is evidence enough that the learning process of AAAS is as neglected by the education systems as the efforts to draw in out of school children. This again is a situation likely to affect the learning process of the SC, ST, DTNT students who are the most vulnerable students.

(ix) Suggestions for refinement of SLSM developed by SCERT

When asked for suggestion for improvement of SLSM developed by the MSCERT two teachers were satisfied with its overall quality but two others were not so and wanted the SLSM to be redesigned for better results with the AAA students. This again is a very important inclusionary component for retaining and promoting students from the most vulnerable communities of the society.

(x) AAA Students difficulties faced while learning

Various difficulties faced by the age appropriate students is highlighted in the following table.

Table - AAA students difficulties faced while learning

Sr. No.	Nature of difficulties	Pune	Beed	Total	Percent
1.	Language not understand	00	03	03	27.27
2.	Teaching speed is too fast Can't under-stand - cause of low confidence	03	02	05	45.45
3.	S.C.E.R.T. educational aids not received on time	00	00	00	0.00
4.	Lack of confidence	02	00	02	18.18
5.	Faced difficulties with English language lose confidence	01	00	01	9.09
	Total	**06**	**05**	**11**	**100.00**

The above table shows the typical difficulties that could be faced by students coming from difficult socio-economic and educational background. Some students did not understand the school teacher language which could be different and standardized as compare to the students dialects while nearly half the students found the teaching to be too fast leading to lack of understanding and loss of confidence. These obstacles led to a complete lack of confidence, which make the retention of these students a very big challenge under the RTE.

This data also reveals the lack of training or efforts on the part of students to accommodate the learning difficulty level of students admitted under age appropriate category.

(xi) Extra Efforts taken for AAA students by School

The following table gives the responses of the students regarding extra efforts taken for the AAA students.

Table - Extra time given by teacher for learning activities

Sr. No.	Response	Pune	Beed	Total	Percent
1.	Yes	06	04	10	90.90
2.	No	00	01	01	9.10
Total		**06**	**05**	**11**	**100**

As evident from the data over 90% respondents said that the teacher give extra time for the fast-track learning of the AAA students. This proved the teachers commitment towards these students requiring special teaching.

On trying to find the type of extra efforts taken by the teachers to simplify difficult subjects, we received the following responses from the AAA students. Over 54% students said that their teachers gave more time to teach difficult subjects and over 36% students replied that their teachers explained the difficult subjects in simple methods. Over 9% students said that subjects were simplified because their teachers taught with educational aids.

Interestingly over 12 % headmasters from the Pune district and over 15% from Beed said that they arranged for extra teaching periods for the AAA students.

The researcher also asked the teacher about their efforts for AAA students. Four teachers out of twenty-two from Pune district said they completed the appropriate training and arranged extra lectures for AAA students beyond school timing. Two said they used special teaching methods and teaching-learning aids for these students. Four teachers from Beed arranged extra lectures. Over 24% teachers said that they sent slow learning age appropriate class students to the lower class for learning. This is a major infringement of the age appropriate learning for out of school children. This reveals the incompetence, lack of teaching aids and lack of efforts on the part of the teachers and the school to accommodate and teach out of school children in age appropriate classes to maintain peer group learning atmosphere. Such deviation may hurt the dignity, confidence and spirit of learning of the AAA students. Only 8.11% teachers completed special training besides this 2% teachers used special aids and methods while teaching.

(xii) Solutions over problems by AAA students

The researcher asked the AAA students regarding the person they sought help from while learning.

As evident from the data over 45% respondents reported asking their teacher about any difficulty, over 18% students took help from their friend and a similar percent of students consulted their family member. But over 18% respondents did not seek anybodies help. It is evident that majority of the students fight shy of talking about their learning difficulties with their teachers. This shows a clear lack of communication among the teacher and the students lowering confidence levels among these students.

(xii) Favourite subjects of AAA students

The researcher tried to find the favourite subject of AAA students and the responses are as follows:

Among the favourite subject AAA students over 27% students liked English and Marathi and over 9% liked math, drawing, science, history and urdu. This clearly shows extra efforts taken by the English teachers when they realised the difficulties of this subject especially with students from underprivileged educational background.

On asking these students on why they liked particular subjects like English over 27% said they like to speak in English and read English stories and poems. While another 18% said their teacher taught very nicely and 27% like subject because they were taught in their mother tongue.

At the same time when these student were queried about the difficult subjects they faced over 36% said it was Maths, another 27% said that was Science and over 18% thought it was English and Marathi. It is evident that typically math and science has been the nemesis of average students and especially those from the socio-economically backward communities. Only the lower difficulty level of English is a bright spot in the learning process of the AAA students.

Further when these students were queried for the reasons of difficulties with particular subject over 18% replied that they could not understand math's due to difficult formulae and thought English was too difficult. 9% students found it difficult to recall new words in English and over 18% could not understand teaching in Marathi as their mother tongue was Hindi.

(xiv) AAA student's friendship with other students

To identify the social composition of the students friend circle the research enquired about their friends names and tried to socially categorize the friend circle to understand the social inclusiveness among peer groups.

Table - Social category of AAA students' friends

Sr. No.	Students from the category of	Pune	Beed	Total	Percent
1.	Backward class	01	02	03	27.27
2.	Other than backward category	01	00	01	9.09
3.	Backward class and other than backward class both.	02	00	02	18.18
4.	Minority and backward with other than backward class	02	01	03	27.27
5.	Only Muslim friends.	00	02	02	18.18
Total		**06**	**05**	**11**	**100.00**

As observed in this table over 27% students had friends from the backward classes and another 27% had friends from all social categories including the minorities. 18% students had friends from the backward and other than backward social categories. 9% students had friends only from other than backward categories. And 18% students had only Muslim friends. The above data configuration suggests that most of the AAA students had friend circle involving students from all social categories. This is a very good indication of innocent friendship untouched by vagaries of social interest that tend to come up in adulthood.

(xv) AAAS participation in the school activities

Education is a means to develop a holistic personality of the children. That's why only academic learning will not develop all-round personality. It has to be supported by extracurricular and sporting activities. The researcher asked the AAA student about their participation in extracurricular and sporting activities of the school and received responses as follows:

In the extracurricular activities over 54% AAA students participated in all types of activities including speech contest, song competition, gathering and group activities. The remaining students participated in one or the other extracurricular activities. This showed the extra liking and high confidence level of AAA students when dealing with multi-faceted activities demanding personal confidence and team work.

The sport activities also showed the keen participation of the AAA students in sporting activities such as basket ball, langadi, kabbadi and cricket.

The participation of the AAA students in both of the above extra-academic activities highlights the affection for physical indulgent and artistic skills among the students which relates them to the vocational talents and cultural affinities of the underprivileged social communities of the country. So the participation of the SC, ST, DTNT students represented by the AAA students under the RTE has to be strongly initiated, nurtured and flourished for the right to education to be truly socially inclusive.

5.14 School Management Committee (SMC)

The school management committee has a statutory status which is a major change from the earlier village education committees whose decision were only advisory in nature. The SMC represents community participation and responsibility towards the education of the village children through the village schools. The SMC is composed of women parents, local government representative members of backward communities and also students representative making it a very a socially inclusive and accountable endeavor of the RTE act. So it would be best if the SMC are made compulsory even in the private unaided schools since they are also participating in the greater social objective of universalisation of elementary education. Further the mandatory nature of the SMCs shall make the private unaided school socially and financially accountable.

5.15 Expectation of parents and students from the school

Under the right to free and compulsory education the parents and students expectations from the school is a matter that we probed. Following are the responses:

As the data shows over 61% from Beed and over 20% and over 3% students from Pune wants individualised attention for the students from the teacher. Over 16% 8th standards students 31% 9th standard students from Pune and over 36% 8th standard students, 15% 9th standard student and 20% AAA students from Beed expected facilities like a ground, extra class rooms, compound wall, purified water, school bus, free educational material and organisation of sports activities. Over 13% parents from Pune and 7% parents from Beed were obviously concerned about academics and accepted more periods for the students with examinations. Then again 13% parents and 10% 9th standard students from Pune along with 7% 9th standard students from Beed accepted teachers to teach as per student's capacity and use PPT for the same. Over 6% parents and 3% 8th standard students from Pune along with 3% 8th standard students and 15% 9th standard students wanted the school toilets to be clean and reduce weight of the school bag. Just 2% 8th standard students from Pune and 5% 8th standard students from Beed accepted arrangement of study tours from the school. Just over 4% 8th standard students from Pune wanted punishment to the students to be stopped. Finally a huge 46% parents, 67% 8th standard students, 57% 9th standard students and a total 100% AAA students have no expectations whatsoever from the school.

It is interesting to note that about half the surveyed students and parents from both Pune and Beed do not have any exceptions from the school. This could be because either the schools have drastically improved qualitatively under the RTE or they are not feeling any significant changes in the school setup even under the implementation of the RTE and so are not expecting anything better.

Table - Expectation from Teachers and School

Sr. No.	Response	Pune				Beed			
		Parents	Students 8th std.	Students 9th	Students AAAS	Parents	Students 8th std.	Students 9th	Students AAAS
1	There is no expectation.	07 (46.67)	72 (67.29)	11 (57.89)	06 (100)	03 (23.08)	48 (53.33)	07 (53.86)	02 (40)
2	Teachers should give individual attention to the students.	03 (20)	04 (3.74)	00 (00)	00 (00)	08 (61.54)	00 (00)	00 (00)	00 (00)
3	Extra & more lectures should be arrange for students, need exam	02 (13.33)	00 (00)	00 (00)	00 (00)	01 (7.69)	00 (00)	00 (00)	00 (00)
4	Teachers have to teach as per students capacity and must use PPT for teaching	02 (13.33)	00 (00)	02 (10.53)	00 (00)	00 (00)	00 (00)	01 (7.69)	00 (00)
5	Ground should be available, Bus, class rooms, Compound, Purified water, Free educational material and organize Sports activities	00 (00)	18 (16.82)	06 (31.58)	00 (00)	00 (00)	33 (36.67)	02 (15.38)	01 (20)
6	Toilet should be cleaned, weight of school bags has to reduce	01 (6.67)	04 (3.74)	00 (00)	00 (00)	00 (00)	03 (3.33)	02 (15.38)	00 (00)
7	Arrange study tour	00 (00)	03 (2.80)	00 (00)	00 (00)	00 (00)	05 (5.56)	00 (00)	00 (00)
8	No punishment to the students	00 (00)	05 (4.67)	00 (00)	00 (00)	00 (00)	00 (00)	00 (00)	00 (00)
9	No Response	00 (00)	01 (0.94)	00 (00)	00 (00)	01 (7.69)	01 (1.11)	01 (7.69)	02 (40)
	Total	**15 (100)**	**107 (100)**	**19 (100)**	**06 (100)**	**13 (100)**	**90 (100)**	**13 (100)**	**05 (100)**

Chapter - 6

Suggestions on Changes to Implementation of RTE

The fieldwork probe of the implementation of the right to education act and its interface with the scheduled castes and tribes students has produced the following major conclusive aspects among others.

I.

(i) Awareness about the Right to Education (RTE) Act

Regarding the most basic aspect for successful implementation of the RTE is the simple awareness about it with the most important stakeholders of the school i.e. teachers, parents and SMC members. Shockingly over 5% teachers, over 21% SMC members and over 46% parents were simply not aware of the RTE. Teachers not knowing about RTE in inexcusable. Now after over ten years of implementation of the RTE act if such basics are weak the state education machinery, the school systems and the civil society has to go on an overdrive for creating awareness through various publicity campaign and also today's ICT connectivity. Even the school teachers who undertake annual survey for out of school children could be assigned with the work of spreading awareness about the RTE in the remotest village homes.

The scheduled caste and scheduled tribe communities are beyond communication reach given their lower literacy levels and low enthusiasm about formal education due to its irrelevance and the need of more working hands at home. These micro and macro level reasons of educational exclusion of these communities need to be addressed over time.

(ii) Age Limit for the RTE

Section 3 of the RTE act provides to every child of the age of six to fourteen years the right to free and compulsory education in a neighbourhood school till the completion of elementary education. However, in urban India the elementary education starts with the age of two and a half years of age. The schools take the kids in pre-nursery if they are three years of age. A child who has an early schooling since the age of 3 will be far ahead from the child who enters the school at the age of 6.The ability of participation of SC and ST students in pre-primary schooling is extremely unlikely, especially in rural and remote areas due to socio-economic obstacles. Other students, especially urban based, get an opportunity to participate in pre-primary education, giving them a head start to tackle proper schooling. Therefore, the act does not take care of the students of age below six. The maximum limit of 14 years for free and compulsory education is also a hindrance to the entrance of SC and ST students to further and higher education. At age 14 a student passes only 8th standard and with the no-detention policy in place the likelihood of the child, due to ill-preparation, going on to secondary and later higher education is quite low. So the upper age limit should be extended to sixteen years i.e. 10 standard. This will increase chances of backward class students' entrance in to the domain of higher education.

(iii) Admission Process under RTE

(a) Screening Test

In this most important stage of entry for free education the admission process plays an important role defined by conduct of screening or entrance test, necessity of essential documents for admission and demand of charges for the admission by the schools. Over 34% students, 32% parents and shockingly 18% headmasters said that screening test was conducted for admission to their school. Screening or entrance test are the biggest obstacles to entry of SC and ST students in to primary education given their socio-economic status, illiteracy, lack of family educational background along with lack of confidence and preparation level of the child.

(b) **Documents for Admission**

The RTE states that no child can be denied admission even if she/he cannot produce any of the necessary documents for admission in the school. It is interesting that in the surveyed schools only 4 admissions were done without any documents whatsoever. Possession of various necessary documents is a difficult proposition for parents and students from the backward communities due to illiteracy and primacy of daily livelihood activities. So it is a matter of publicity in the society and sensitisation of school authorities regarding low prioritisation of documents for admissions under RTE to make it socially inclusive.

(c) **Admission Fees**

Over 15% private aided schools charged one or the other fees to students which included one school charging admission fee, another charging for travel to school and three schools collecting exam fees. This is a gross violation of the right to free education between six to fourteen years as section 2 (n) (ii) provides for free education in unaided schools receiving aid or grant to meet whole or part of its expenses from the appropriate government or the local authority. This willful breach of law by private aided schools exposes the students from vulnerable communities such as the SC and ST towards dropping out of schooling.

Over 19% private unaided schools charged fees up to upper primary level which included two schools charging admission fees, one school charging exam fees and three schools charging the whole consolidated fees. This also is a gross violation of the right to free education and exposes the profiteering tendencies of the un-aided schools along with their reluctance to accommodate 25% disadvantaged and weaker section students from the neighbourhood even when the state reimbursement of the expenses of the 25% quota students is legally provided for. Surprisingly one Municipal Corporation school has charged for admission and exam fees in total violation of the act. This highlights complete ignorance on the part of government schools that need to be well informed and trained for successful implementation of the RTE. The tribal department, Z.P., Nagarpalika and Poona cantonment board schools have all followed the fundamentals of the RTE by not charging any fees whatsoever.

The field data revealed some schools to have charged various fees in total contravention of the right to free and compulsory act. This especially goes against the SC and ST students and proves to be a socially excluding obstacle. There should be heavy financial penalty to such errant schools with provision for de-recognition of schools committing multiple infringements on this count.

(d) Number of admission and vacant seats under 25% reservation quota in schools

The 25% reservation quota for the disadvantaged groups and weaker sections is possibly the most radical provision of the right to education as a step towards social inclusion. The efficacy of its implementation can be seen from the number of admission and vacancies of the 25% quota of the surveyed schools.

15% headmasters from Beed and 27% from Pune said that their schools had vacancies under the 25% quota admission. A huge 84% did not reply to this query.

The researcher noticed the lack of awareness about the admission under the 25% reservation quota in all the schools. The researcher asked the headmasters and teachers about number of admissions and vacant seats under 25% reservation quota in the current academic year. Twenty-one (63.64%) headmasters did not give any responses which included 11 headmasters from Pune and 10 from Beed district. Further, the researcher asked about the vacant seats under the reservation quota and over 15% headmasters acknowledged having vacancies under the 25% quota. And over 84% headmasters did not respond to this query.

(e) Admissions and vacant seats under reservation quotas

Researcher asked the headmasters about the admissions and vacant seats under the 25% reservation quota. 61.11% headmasters from Pune did not give any responses. In Pune from 6 unaided private schools 50% schools gave admission to 58 students from the disadvantaged and weaker sections under the 25% reservation quota. While in Beed none of the headmasters gave any response to the issue of 25% quota admission. Here all three unaided schools did not report any admissions under the 25% reservation quota.

It is very clear from the above data that the admissions under the 25% reservation quota for the neighbourhood backward and poor students are not implemented well. This could prove to be a huge implementation failure in social inclusion of the RTE act.

(f) Schools action if fewer applications for admission under 25% quota

The data survey showed that some schools did not republish the advertisement for 25% quota admissions if they were not filled up in the first round. While some schools simply opened the vacant 25% quota admissions to be filled by the general quota students. These infringements reek of non-desire to accommodate the deprived students under this quota. It also raises suspicions of letting out admissions for illegal, financial or other favors. This significant fault hurting the socially deprived students needs to be addressed by strict monitoring and making provision of heavy financial penalty in the act.

(g) Parents awareness about the 25% admissions reservation quota

The survey showed that nearly 40% parents were unaware of the provision of 25% quota for admissions of the disadvantaged and weaker section students. This calls for rectification from the government agencies and civil societies with enhanced all-round publicity and the school survey teachers imparting home to home information of the same.

(h) Admission Denied by the schools

Considering the 100% non-reportage/compliance of admissions under the reservation quota from Beed and 50% from Pune, we consider it as the denial of admission under this quota by the schools as reported by the parents identified with their social category. Just over 7% parents including over 3% schedule caste parents reported denial of admission by the school under the 25% reservation quota. The reasons reported by the parents for being denied admissions included parents being uneducated or having no knowledge of English.

(iv) Fee reimbursement

Inadequate or irregular or non reimbursement of the per capita student's expenditure by the government infringes on the most basic provision of access for the disadvantaged groups and weaker section students under the right to education act. If the government, with provision of the RTE act, has forced the unaided private schools to fill up 25% of their seats with deprived neighbourhood students it is the duty of the government to reimburse the actual amount of expenditure per student that varies with the quality each unaided private school displays. Reimbursing these schools with average government per student expenditure is not only unjust to these schools but creates huge obstacles for the neighbourhood socio-economically deprived students to be accommodated socially and educationally in the school atmosphere.

(v) Students under 25% quota and issue of social distance

The 25% reservation quota is for the disadvantaged groups comprising of the scheduled castes and tribes students and the weaker sections that is the economically poor students. We have a history of social differentiation with the scheduled castes and tribes, so the matter of probing social distance among the SC, ST and other students is significant. Over 62% teachers replied that there was no social distance maintained with the SC, ST students but significantly, one teacher acknowledged that social distance was maintained against the SC, ST students.

The issue of social relationships on caste basis is very delicate and burdened with social pressure, so it is very significant that even then one teacher said that social distance which ultimately meant social discrimination was prevalent against SC, ST students. The issue of social distance/discrimination is one highlighting factor that goes against the assimilative or integrative proposition of SC, ST and poor students coming under the 25% quota with the other relatively affluent students of the private unaided schools. Apart from the 25% quota students not matching up to the over and above necessary expenses of the private unaided schools, the maintenance of social distance/discrimination keeps the SC, ST students individually and communally alienated from the mainstream culture of the private un-aided schools. Considering the private unaided schools resentment against filling up the 25% quota seats, the untimely and in-adequate reimbursement of the quota admission from the government and the denial of cultural assimilation of the students by the school systems and the other students warrants a major amendment to the RTE act. And that is of completely withdrawing the provision of 25% quota for the disadvantaged and weaker section students. This conclusion was forced on us due to the huge implementation issues of this quota and the incessant resentment and alienation of the management and affluent students of the private unaided schools against the students from neighbourhood deprived communities.

The issue of social distance can be resolved by a healthy and dynamic relationship between the teacher and the students for a holistic development of knowledge and skills among the students. But as discussed earlier a socially prejudiced mindset carried by a teacher, partially evident from our survey data, makes the SC, ST students, coming under the 25% admission quota, all the more vulnerable to developing an inferiority complex leading to academic decay or ultimate school drop-out/push out.

Public approach is the original approach to education of societies across the world. It stands for carrying over the culture encompassing the traditions and evolving with modernity and its tools of utility. Its aim was and is individual excellence but in the overall framework of public interest. Traditionally in this public approach for education the social studies have been given as much importance as the sciences and maths in pursuit of a balance between individual and technical excellence, but for the overall interest of the framework of social relations and the community at large. Profit motive had limited space. Now especially after the onset of the process of globalisation, liberalisation and privatisation education is fully commoditised. Private initiative, pursuit of knowledge inclined towards employability and entrepreneurship is not a bad idea. It is a need of the contemporary market driven society. This leads to individualism and utilitarianism with greater profit motive and ultimately to competition starting in primary education itself. The simple reasoning being- the more ones spends on private education the more one is under pressure to achieve the returns, especially financial through profit. The public approach of education is more holistic and even when the ultimate motive is of individual excellence and entrepreneurship for financial gains, even if in a subtle manner, molded for overall community prosperity. Democracy and modernity along with globalisation demand commoditisation and privatisation of education for competition and utilitarian excellence but our country is still lagging behind on the socio-economic indicators of income, social justice and industrialisation. The state in India still has a lot of work to do as a welfare state so instead of enforcing educational upliftment of the backward and poor classes on private educational initiatives it should delete provisions such as the 25% reservation quota in private un-aided schools and instead make adequate financial allocations for education and raise the overall quality of public schools in India.

(vi) Special Efforts for the educational improvement of students from disadvantaged groups and weaker sections

Over 48% teachers took special efforts to improve the educational quality of the students from disadvantaged groups and weaker sections. However, it is shocking to note that over 13% teachers did not take any special efforts and over 37% teachers simply did not respond to this query showing a tendency of neglect of or prejudice against students from difficult socio-economic background. This is a matter of not just extra training but motivation and social sensitisation for the teachers by government agencies, school management and credible NGO interventions.

(vii) Grievance and Redressal

Grievance redressal mechanism is setup by the government to address and give justice to parents/students in the case of denial of their right to free and compulsory education. The mechanism for this redressal is the government machinery represented by the education department locally right up to the apex institution of the national commission for protection for child rights (NCPCR), in an ascending appellate order.

It is interesting to note that the state grievance redressal mechanism is mandated and expected to give justice for aggrieved parents/students against their own government branch/education department. It is a matter of conjecture whether a state grievance redressal mechanism can dispense justice to parents/students with action against the states own service provider agencies viz. the education department. Actually the grievance redressal mechanism should be as autonomous as our independent judiciary to really dispense justice for grievances under the RTE, especially to the students from the disadvantaged groups and weaker sections.

Parents should be allowed to register a complaint for denial of admission by any school to the local education officer, SMC chairperson or to the state commission for protection of child rights. Three schools from the surveyed districts had denied admissions under the 25% reservation quota but no parents had registered any complaint to any of the concerned authorities. It means the parents were unaware about the avenues of grievance redressal provided under the RTE act.

The grievance and redressal mechanism especially at the local, city or district level where it is manned by the educational authorities need to be revisited. Along with the educational department mechanism, the local credible NGOs working in the field of education should be legally involved to give justice to incidents of grievance regarding admission and other issues under the RTE act. Besides multifaceted publicity of the grievance redressal mechanism with communication connectivity should be created right up to the village level for easy access to justice for all regarding their right to education.

(viii) Age appropriate admitted children

The most important objective of the right to education act is universalisation of elementary education. To achieve this objective the pulling in of out of school children of the cities and the villages is most essential. Across 33 surveyed schools the data reveals that only 11 out of school children were admitted in the age appropriate admission category. Incidentally all of them belong to the backward castes including from the scheduled caste, the de-notified and nomadic tribes and minority backward class. This again highlights the issue of social exclusion and the necessity for a more formal and stronger set up to survey the out of school children when the UNESCO *e-atlas on out-of-school children* (OOSC) report states that out of school children in India constituted a huge 17.7 million out of a total of 124 million worldwide. So it is evident that survey, identification, accommodation and assimilation of out of school children is a huge challenge for the school system, local community and educational administration that needs to be addressed because effectively this issue affects social inclusion which is the most important objective of the RTE act.

(ix) Continuous and Comprehensive Evaluation (CCE)

The CCE is a very significant provision of the RTE as it evaluates the academic, physical and as well as emotional aspects of the students for a holistic learning. But for a more effective implementation of the CEE the government, the school system and relevant NGOs with credibility need to put in far more resources and training especially for the teacher who is the core coordinator of the process of CCE. Far more and varied learning aids and ideas for individual and team learning need to be developed and provided. The teacher needs to undergo rigorous and continuous in-service training so as to be able to understand and provide a learning which covers the intellectual, emotional and physical aspects of the students. Moreover, CCE is just an evaluative process. The RTE seems to have, if not totally overlooked, at least given far less attention to a comprehensive curriculum. Because only a comprehensive curriculum would warrant a continuous and comprehensive evaluation. The CCE is only a structure without the substance for want of a comprehensive curriculum. A comprehensive curriculum would need to comprise of varied pedagogies, interdisciplinary curriculum, intellectual as well as manual-skills learning with dignity of labour and an inclusive social atmosphere for a holistic learning. The different subjects of social studies, sciences, maths and languages need to be taught in an interwoven manner for awakening a holistic thought process in the young minds of the students. Curriculum is the heart of education which needs to represent the socially defined occupational variation and the school neighbourhood domain occupational profile to make it relevant and productive, that to in a comfortable local dialect. This approach would warrant a different paradigm of pedagogy based on learning while doing, being given more primacy over memorisation and presentation skills which have traditionally been the weak points of the backward class students leading to exclusion from the educational system. Our prime vocation being agriculture along with the basics of social sciences like Sociology, Politics, Psychology, Economics and Anthropology needs to be interwoven with the sciences at the elementary level for a holistic outcome of knowledge laced with skills for a socially inclusive education. So the RTE needs to accommodate such comprehensive curriculum to be complimented to an effective evaluative process.

(x) No-detention policy

Significantly a majority of teachers and significant number of parents feel that the learning process is affected due to the no-detention policy. This raises question marks on the substance and structure of the learning process under the RTE. This underlines that the no-detention policy has removed fear from the process of learning, but the learning process without a comprehensive and relevant curriculum has failed to enthuse joy in the learning process.

It is astonishing that a huge majority of headmaster and significant number of teachers wanted to get back the provision of detaining students. This is the biggest contravention of the most important provision i.e. no-detention policy of the RTE act. As discussed earlier where it was mentioned that the CCE was incomplete without a comprehensive curriculum, similarly the no-detention policy is incomplete without corroborative inputs of teacher training, multiple pedagogies, interdisciplinary and relevant curriculum, comprehensive evaluation and adequate resources for learning aids and practical's along with dynamic interaction of the school with socio-cultural, commercial and industrial entities of the school neighbourhood. It needs to be underlined that schools are for learning purpose and not for screening out students. It is a well documented fact that school dropouts and class repeating students mostly comprise of the scheduled tribes, the scheduled castes, the DTNTs and the girl child. The yesteryears policy of detention has been a nemesis to these students who come from underprivileged backgrounds.

The no-detention policy is a major facilitator for the universalisation of elementary education but here our data exposes that a majority of headmasters and significant number of teachers want the recall of the detention policy. This is a major question mark on the very spirit of opening doors of primary education to all including the SC, ST and others. This is a huge implementation challenge and makes one wonder whether the no-detention policy should be withdrawn for seven years so that the school system and the establishment improves to a level where the question of detention would be irrelevant. This would happen only if radical changes are made as discussed earlier.

Traditionally in India from the ancient times scriptural directives prohibited the backward castes from receiving any education, religious or utilitarian. With global cultural exposure during the British and modern times and the onset of democracy underlined by the fundamental rights of liberty, equality and justice giving the rights to education to all the communities of the country we have a formal education system for the same. Our education system is based on an examination system leading to individualised competition and screening out of individuals not making it to the required mark. As discussed earlier the social, economic and educational background of the SC and ST students have made them major victims along with some others to be failures and drop outs of the schooling system. The right to education while changing this scenario has brought in the provision of no-detention till the 8th standard for all children. Our data reveals that most of the headmaster and teachers along with some parents oppose the no-detention policy. They contend that due to this policy the teachers are not under the pressure to deliver and the students along with their parents, become negligent of studies with the awareness of each child being promoted up to 8th standard with or without the prescribed levels of learning. The government has come up with this provision without the substantial backup for its satisfactory implementation. No-detention policy actually means ensuring all children received the prescribed levels of learning in each class which would require a thorough overhaul of teacher training, pedagogy, curriculum and teaching aids. The teacher needs to be given greater social status, as received in ancient times, far better financial incentive (better than senior college teachers as done in some western countries) and comprehensive and continuous in-service training with greater autonomy and responsibility. The curriculum needs to be relevant especially to the school and regional socio-economic domain. It needs to be interdisciplinary interweaving the sciences and the basics of social sciences along with primary activities like agriculture and vocational skills of the region to make it accommodative of the social diversity of the region. Relevance leads to interest that leads to understanding and to ultimate knowledge outputs. Our primary basis of memorisation and presentation for learning has to be complimented by practical activities by a dynamics between the mental skills and manual efficacies. This whole process will make detention irrelevant and obsolete. But given the rate of change of our educational process this radical change is too big a task for the Indian educational system. So the via media could be that the detention policy should be brought back at the 6th standard level. This step is already in the pipeline on the advice of the Central Advisory Board of Education (CABE). This prescription would look socially regressive as it undermines the socio-economic and educational handicaps of the backward caste students but the fact today that large number of students fail in 9th standard because of being promoted up to 8th standard without the prescribed level of learning cannot be overlooked. This simply is due to incompetence of the school system to ensure no-detention along with prescribed levels of learning. The failures of the 9th standard level among others obviously include large numbers of SC and ST students. So in the given situation it is better to go back to the detention policy so that all stakeholders of the school system shall again take troubles and responsibilities of learning. But this can only be a temporary step back for say a period of seven years. No-detention is the ideal when all the above prescriptions are implemented to make learning a relevant and joyful process making detention completely irrelevant.

(xi) School Management Committee (SMC)

The school management committee has a statutory status which is a major change from the earlier village education committees whose decision were only advisory in nature. The SMC represents community participation and responsibility towards the education of the village children through the village schools. The SMC is composed of women parents, local government representative, members of backward communities and also students representative making it a very a socially inclusive and accountable endeavour of the RTE act. So it would be best if the SMC are made compulsory even in the private unaided schools since they are also participating in the greater social objective of universalisation of elementary education. Further the mandatory nature of the SMCs shall make the private unaided school socially and financially accountable.

II. Suggestions for more effective implementation of the RTE act –

(a) The age group for free and compulsory education should be 3 to 16 under RTE. Even Sri Lanka, a neighborhood developing country has provision of free and compulsory education to children between 5 and 14 years of age.

(2) Admission entry point for free and compulsory education should be at any class level till 8th standard. Students who miss out an admission at first standard level are in danger of staying out of elementary education or starting elementary education a year late. This is especially significant for the educational inclusion of the SC and ST students.

(3) Some school functionaries were not aware of the RTE provision of granting admission to students even if they did not posses any or all essential documents. This provision is extremely crucial and helpful for social inclusion of the SC and ST students. The government machinery needs to impart basic information of the RTE provisions to all the stakeholders of the RTE process.

(4) Screening test or interview for admission under RTE is the most socially exclusionary obstacle to the education of the SC and ST students. Heavy financial penalty should be imposed on first time defaulting schools while there should be RTE provision for no-recognition of schools which frequently faulted on this count.

(5) For the schools which charged various fees, in total contravention of the RTE act, there should be provision of heavy financial penalty along with provision for de-recognition of schools committing multiple infringements on this count.

(6) The Continuous and Comprehensive Evaluation needs to be complimented by a comprehensive curriculum based on variations in pedagogies, interdisciplinary curriculum and dynamics of mental and manual skills. The processes of memorisation and presentation need to be only one aspect of evaluation among others. Evaluation is not substantive without comprehensive curriculum.

(7) There is a need of expert training on CCE to all the persons who have direct concern with school education, especially the Headmasters and teachers.

(8) Infringement of RTE provisions to be redressed maximum at the education officer level and one next authority above at district level.

(9) Grievance redressal committee to be formed comprising education officer, civil society representative including NGOs working for RTE. Their decision to be final and binding.

(10) Centralisation of 25% admission process with the education office at district level needs to be done reducing role of non-compliance by private un-aided schools on the issues of 25% quota admission among others.

(11) Some schools simply opened the vacant 25% quota admissions to be filled by the general quota students. These infringements reek of non-desire to accommodate the deprived students under this quota. It also gives doubts of giving out admissions for illegal, financial or other favours. This significant fault hurting the socially deprived students needs to be addressed by strict monitoring and making provision of heavy financial penalty.

(12) 25% reservation quota should be applicable for any class between Ist to VIIIth standards.

(13) Awareness of the 25% admission quota with parents especially rural, remote and from deprived communities is of essence. The government agencies and the civil society entities have to enhance all-round publicity of the 25% quota provision and the school survey teachers imparting home-to-home information of the same.

(14) Most of the private unaided schools are opposing the admission under 25% reservations quota due to the defective government reimbursement system. For effective implementation of the 25% seats in private schools, there is a need to ensure a fair selection process, adequate and timely reimbursement from the state and a transparent monitoring and evaluation system.

(15) Provision of heavy financial penalty and or jail term for infringement of the right to education in the RTE act.

(16) With so many implementation issues, as discussed in the conclusions and main analysis, it is best recommended that the 25% admission quota needs to be withdrawn. The provision of 25% reservation in private schools is not available in any other country except India. But for the time being the above course corrections may be implemented to

make it effective in the interests of the disadvantaged and weaker section students.

(17) As discussed in details in the main analysis and in the conclusion regarding issue of no-detention policy it is better to go back to the detention policy so that all stake holders of the school system shall again take troubles and responsibilities of learning. But this can only be a temporary step back for say a period of seven years. No-detention is the ideal when all recommendations made earlier are implemented to make learning a relevant and joyful process making detention completely irrelevant.

(18) Continuous and comprehensive before and in-service training for teachers should comprise varied pedagogies, child psychology, advance learning aids, ICT, social sensitisation and interdisciplinary understanding and teaching.

(19) Committed provision of personnel including school teachers to spot and collect out of school children.

(20) Additional and committed set-up with extra training and teaching resources along with financial incentive to the teacher.

(21) Schooling and social sensitisation of SMC members needs to be undertaken with vigour.

(22) Provision of SMC should be compulsory to private un-aided schools to bring about social and financial accountability in the RTE endeavour of universalisation of elementary education.

(23) Significant number of teachers did not take any special efforts for the improvement of the students from disadvantaged groups and weaker sections and over 37% teachers simply did not respond to this query showing a tendency of neglect of or prejudice against students from difficult socio-economic background. This is a matter of not just extra training but motivation and social sensitisation for the teachers by government agencies, school management and credible NGO interventions.

(24) To make a success of the implementation of the RTE act the government has to allocate at least 6% of its GDP for education as recommended far back by the Kothari commission in 1966. For additional resources for education

the government may collect and redirect the corporate social responsibility funds of private industries to the education sector and also encourage any private entity to donate for this educational endeavour.

Bibliography

1. Arvind Kumar,*'Law and Dalits 'Social Inclusion in India*', article accessed from - http://focusglobalreporter. com/article17.asp
2. Bhan, Sujata & Suzanne Rodricks (2012), '*Indian Perspective on Child's Right to Education*' paper published in the procedia-social and behavioral sciences 69 (2012) 367 – 376, available online at www.sciencedirect.com
3. Chowdhury, Rishad (2010), "*The road less travelled': Article 21A and The Fundamental Right to Primary Education in India*" Paper published in Indian Journal of Constitutional Law.
4. Department of School Education and Literacy, MHRD (2010), '*Report on Committee on Implementation of the Right of children to free an Compulsory Education Act, 2009*'.
5. Department of Economics and social Affairs (2009), report published on '*Creating an Inclusive Society: Practical Strategies to Promote Social Integration*'.
6. Dhaatri Resource Center for Women and Children (2011), '*A Report on the Status of Primary Education of Adivasi Children in Andhra Pradesh and Orissa in the Context of Right to Education Act 2009*', report submitted to Andhra Pradesh.
7. *Education for All Towards Quality with Equity* (2014), report by NUEPA, New Delhi.
8. *Education For All: Status and Trends* (2012), National University of Educational Planning and Administration 17-B, Sri Aurobindo Marg, New Delhi.
9. *Educational Statistics at a glance 2013-14*, MHRD, New Delhi and *Elementary Education in India progress towards UEE*, DISE 2009-10, NUEPA, New Delhi.
10. *Educational Statistics at a Glance*, MHRD: New Delhi, 2014.
11. Government of Maharashtra (1982), '*Babasaheb Ambedkar : Writings and Speeches*', Vol. 2, p. 62.
12. Gursharan Singh Kainth (2012), '*Right to Education Act in India*' article published in The India Post dated 12th Feb. 2012 -http://www.theindiapost.com/articles/right-to-education-act-in-india/
13. Gupta, Shantanu (2009), '*What are the different strategies and approaches to realize Right to Education (RTE) in India?*', Institute of Development Studies (IDS).
14. http://mpsp.maharashtra.gov.in/upload/Advertisement/00%20Maharashtra%20Profile%202014-15%20Complete.pdf
15. http://nces.ed.gov/programs/coe/indicator_cmd.asp

16. http://shodhganga.inflibnet.ac.in/bitstream/10603/8116/12/12_chapter%203.pdf
17. http://timesofindia.indiatimes.com/india/1-4-million-Indian-children-aged-6-11-out-of-school-Unesco/articleshow/37929697.cms
18. http://www.census2011.co.in/census/district/361-bid.html
19. http://www.worldbank.org/en/topic/socialdevelopment/brief/social-inclusion
20. https://en.wikipedia.org/wiki/Beed
21. https://en.wikipedia.org/wiki/Beed_district
22. http://www.census2011.co.in/census/district/359-pune.html
23. I. Narendra Kumar and S. Siva Prasad (2012), '*Right to Education and equal Opportunity in India*' In: Rao Pulla, (ed.) *Right to Education as An Inclusive Policy*, New Delhi: ABD Publishers.
24. Jha, J., Ghatak, N., Mahendiran, S., and Bakshi, S. (2013, February). '*Implementing the Right to Education Act 2009: the Real Challenges*' (a discussion paper). Centre for Budget and Policy Studies, Bangalore, India.
25. Jha, Praveen and Parvati, Pooja (2010), '*Right to Education Act 2009: Critical Gaps and Challenges*' article published in Economic and Political Weekly, Vol. XLV No. 13.
26. Joshi, S.K., (2013), '*Journey of Right to Education: A Historical Perceptive*' article in an International peer reviewed scholarly research journal for interdisciplinary studies, Vol. II/IX.
27. Juneja, Nalini (2003), '*Constitutional Amendments to make Education a fundamental Right Issues for a follow-up Legislation*', New Delhi: NUEPA.
28. Kabeer, Naila, Geetha B. Nambissan and Subrahmanian, Ramya (2003), '*Child Labour and the right to education in South Asia Needs versus Rights?*' (ed.), New Delhi: Sage Publications.
29. Khumtiya, Debbarma (2011), '*Challenges in Implementation of Right to Free and Compulsory Education Act, 2009: A Critical Analysis of India with special focus on Karnataka*' report submitted to Fiscal Policy Institute, Bangalore, Finance Department, Government of Karnataka.
30. Malik, Krishna Pal (2012), '*Right to Elementary Education*', Allahabad Law Agency, Allahabad.
31. Mohapatra, Tanuja (2011) '*Tribes of Odisha: Issues of social inclusion, exclusion and cultural assimilation*' article published in Bodhy: An interdisciplinary Journal, 5, ISSN: 2091-0479.
32. Nayak,Harat Kumar (2012), '*Implementing Clause 12 of the Right to Education Act 2009 in Udaipur District of Rajasthan, India: Letting Disadvantaged Children Down?*', International Institute of Social Studies, P.O. Box 2977 2502 LT The Hague, The Netherlands.
33. Nabin Eawal, '*Social Inclusion and Exclusion: A Review*', Dhaulagiri Journal of Sociology and Anthropology Vol: 2.
34. Niranjanaradhya, V. P. and Jha, Abhinav (2013), '*Right of Children to Free and Compulsory Education ACT- Miles to Go... A Case Study of a Gram Panchayat*' Bangalore: Books for Change International Publishing House.

35. Niranjanaradhya and Aruna Kashyap (2006), *'The 'Fundamentals' of the Fundamental Right to Education in India',* United Nations Educational, Scientific and Cultural Organisation, Centre for Child and the Law, National Law School of India University, Bangalore.
36. Ojha Seema S. (2013), '*Implementing Right to Education: Issues and Challenges*'.
37. Planning Department Government of Maharashtra (2013), '*Report of the High Level Committee on the Balanced Regional Development Issues in Maharashtra'.*
38. Puar, Surjit Singh (2012), '*Right to Education Act: A Critical Analysis*' article published in International Journal of Educational and Psychological Research (IJEPR) Volume 1, Issue 2.
39. R. Govinda, Madhumita Bandyopadhyay (2008), *Access to Elementary Education in India Country analytical Review*, New Delhi : NUEPA.
40. R.Govind, *'Implementing Right to Education Act in India: Major Issues and Challenges',* National Institute of Educational Planning and Administration India.
41. Rao, G. Syamala (2012), '*Significance of Right to Education in* India'. in Rao, Pulla (ed.), *Right to education as an Inclusive Policy*, New Delhi:ABD Publishers.
42. Rao, Pulla (2012), '*Right to Education as An Inclusive Policy*'(Ed.), New Delhi, ABD Publishers.
43. Rao, Syamala G. (2012), *Significance of Right to Education,* in Rao, Pulla (ed.) Right to Education an Inclusive Policy, ABD Publishers, New Delhi.
44. Rustagi, Preet (2012), '*Challenges for Right to Education in India*' India development report New Delhi (u.a.): Oxford University press, ZDB-ID 20232986 – Vol. 7, 2012.
45. S.Kumar (2010), '*School Education in India Quality Improvement Techniques*' (ed.) New Delhi: New Century Publications.
46. Sarkar Chanchal Chand (2013),*'Right of Children to free and Compulsory Education Act, 2009 and its Implementation*', article published in India Infrastructure Report 2012, New Delhi: IDFC Foundation.
47. *School Education in India, Flash Statistics 2015*, National University of Educational Planning and Administration, New Delhi.
48. *Selected Educational Statistics 2004-05*, MHRD, GOI, New Delhi, p. III & Educational Statistics at a Glance (2014), MHRD, GOI, New Delhi.
49. Sharma, Amit & Chunawala, Sugra - '*Marching Towards Inclusive Education: Are We Prepared for Inclusive Science Education?*' http://episteme.hbcse.tifr.res.in/index.php/episteme5/5/paper/download /127/20
50. Sharma, Mool Chand (2013), '*Right to Education - Imperative for Progress'*, Alahabad: Universal Law Publishers.
51. Singh, Srishti (2014), '*Inclusive Primary Education: A Means to Social Inclusion?*' working paper for summer internship for Center fir Civil Society
52. Singh, Devendra (2013), '*Child Labour and Right to Education'*, Central Law Publication, 107, Darbhanga Castle, Allahabad.

53. Sonowal C.J. (2008) '*Indian Tribes. and Issue of social inclusion and* Exclusion', Article published in stud Tribes, Tribls, 6(2)
54. *The Gazette of India*, Ministry of Human Resource Development (Department of School Education and Literacy), New Delhi, Notification, 10th September, 2012.
55. Thote Prashant, L. Mathew and Rathoure (2013), '*Right to Education Act: An Anaysis of Teacher Awareness in central India*' research paper published in International Journal of Advanced Research (2013), Volume 1, Issue 3.
56. Tilak, J B G (2012), '*Right to Homeschooling vs Right to Education*', article published in Economic and Political Weekly, Vol. XLVII No. 41.
57. *Twelfth Five Year Plan (2012-17): Faster, More Inclusive & Sustainable Growth*, Volume I.
58. *U-DISE - Elementary Education in India: Trends* 2005-06 to 2014-15.
59. Uma (2013), '*Right to Education (RTE): A Critical Appraisal*', article published in IOSR Journal of Humanities and Social Sciences (JHSS), Vol. 6, Issue-4.
60. Yadav, R. P. (2013), '*Right to Education*', New Delhi: Raj Publications.
61. Nabin Eawal, *Social Inclusion and Exclusion: A Review*, Dhaulagiri Journal of Sociology and Anthropology, Vol. 2, pp. 161,162.
62. Sonowal, C.J. (2008), *Indian Tribes, and Issue of social inclusion and Exclusion*, Article published in stud Tribes, Tribals, 6(2) pp. 123,124.
63. Twelfth Five Year Plan (2012-17): Faster, More Inclusive & Sustainable Growth, Volume I.
64. Mohapatra, Tanuja (2011), '*Tribes of Odisha: Issues of social inclusion, exclusion and cultural assimilation*' article published in Bodhy: An interdisciplinary Journal, 5, ISSN: 2091-0479.
65. http://www.worldbank.org/en/topic/socialdevelopment/brief/social-inclusion
66. Department od Economics and Social Affairs (2009), report published on '*Creating an Inclusive Society: Practical Strategies to Promote Social Integration*'.
67. Arvind Kumar, *Law and Dalits' Social Inclusion in India*, article accessed from - http://focusglobalreporter. com/article17.asp
68. Singh, Srishti (2014), '*Inclusive Primary Education: A Means to Social Inclusion?*' working paper for summer internship for Center for Civil Society.
69. Sharma, Amit & Chunawala, Sugra - '*Marching Towards Inclusive Education: Are We Prepared for Inclusive Science Education?*' article published at http://episteme.hbcse.tifr.res.in/index.php/episteme5/5/paper/download /127/20.

Index

C

D

E

S

T

U